Growing Up North

Morris Bradburn

iUniverse, Inc.
Bloomington

Growing Up North

iUniverse books may be ordered through booksellers or by contacting:

iUniverse
1663 Liberty Drive
Bloomington, IN 47403
www.iuniverse.com
1-800-Authors (1-800-288-4677)

ISBN: 978-1-4620-1894-9 (sc)
ISBN: 978-1-4620-1895-6 (hc)
ISBN: 978-1-4620-1896-3 (ebk)

Library of Congress Control Number: 2011909314

Printed in the United States of America

iUniverse rev. date: 08/04/2011

Acknowledgment

I want to thank the Norway House Cree Nation (KenasoSipi), the helpful staff at the Norway House Band Council Office, the Frontier College Library at Norway House, and the Oxford House Bunibonibee Cree Nation for their help providing information on the histories of their communities, and the people of these communities for their support and encouragement in my writing.

A special thank you to my wife, Becky, who gave me the privacy and encouragement that allowed me to accomplish the writing of this book.

Growing Up North

Chapter 1
Norway House, Manitoba

I HAVE MANY FOND memories of my childhood from when my mother and I visited Grandma Nellie Poker in Norway House, Manitoba. It was during a hot summer day in Norway House, while I was walking by the power-generating building when I saw the local power house operator remove a soft drink from a soft drink cooler. I watched him open the drink as it gave a hissing sound, which aroused my curiosity. He noticed that I was watching him. He put some more coins into the machine and took one more out and offered me the bottled drink that he called Orange Crush. The first gulp I took was the best thing I had ever tasted, and I was hooked. From then on, I used all my allowance money each week to purchase soft drinks from the Hudson's Bay store. That morning was also the first time I tasted a banana and grapes, which I also liked very much. It's strange how some of the first experiences of tastes will always be etched permanently into one's memory.

That same day was also the first time I saw a motor vehicle on wheels. It was being driven across the field near the residential and day schools. It was a half-ton truck that was owned by the Norway House Indian Agent. I felt very fortunate to get a ride on this truck, as I had begged and pestered the driver so much that day that he finally gave in and let me ride in the box. I was so thrilled to ride in that truck that I didn't want the ride to end, and the driver finally threatened to throw me off the truck if I didn't get off when we arrived at the other end of the field, where he had to load some material for a building. This was one of the happiest events of that particular Norway House summer. I was five years old.

When it was near time for me to be born, my mother; my father; and my sister, Nellie, travelled from Oxford House to Norway House by canoe—a distance of 186 kilometres (115.58 miles)—to reach the nearest hospital. I was born at this hospital during the summer of 1944. The hospital was situated on an Indian reservation just north of the Hudson's Bay fort in the area known as Rossville. The reservation was named Rossville in honour of the Hudson's Bay Company's chief factor, Donald Ross, in 1829. My father established a business in the fur trade at Oxford House, which was why we lived there. Everyone at Oxford House spoke Cree, the main dialect of the people. My mother spoke only Cree since she was taught to read and write in the Cree language. My father, on the other hand, spoke both Cree and English; as an orphan, he had been educated in an English school. Everyone who lived in Oxford House and Norway House spoke Cree. The only time English was spoken was when outsiders from the south, such as missionaries and medical personnel, came to our community. Some of the community leaders, including the chief, could speak a little English to get by. We spoke Cree in our home.

Every summer thereafter until I was nine, my mother, my father, and I would travel to Norway House to visit my maternal grandmother Nellie Poker and my mother's large extended family. While there, my father would work at his warehouse in the same community to receive freight for his store at Oxford House, Manitoba. The merchandise he received was shipped from Winnipeg on the lake boats that crossed Lake Winnipeg, the sixth largest freshwater lake in Canada and the eleventh largest freshwater lake in the world. Then it was stored at the warehouse my father had built at Norway House. The freight for the store included food, hardware, clothing, fabrics, and tools. There were also traps and snares that the trappers used to trap their fur for trade. My father would forward this freight to his trading post using many canoes, which were linked together by rope and known as canoe trains. With loaded canoes, the trip to Oxford House, Manitoba, would cover 186 kilometres. Occasionally, the canoe trains were delayed at many of the lake crossings as a result of high winds causing high waves on the lakes. A loaded canoe sat lower in the water, and as a result, only about 15.24 centimetres (6 inches) of it was above the water line.

The Norway House community, located in northern Manitoba, was where my mother was born and where my grandmother, Nellie Poker, lived. I enjoyed the summers in Norway House, as Grandma and every one of my mother's sisters and relatives made my mother, father, and I feel so welcome in their community. I got to meet many cousins, and we became playmates during those summer months, exploring the shores along the community together. We spent most of the summer swimming and playing under the old bridge that crossed the small creek by Grandma's house. Grandma would often take Mom and me visiting other people within the community, and this would sometimes take up most of the afternoon. Mom and I spent a lot of time visiting her sisters. Sometimes they would all come over to Grandma's house for the day, and Grandma's yard would be a beehive of activity as all the kids played games together. Sometimes my mother allowed me to go with one of her sisters and their children to the local store or out to visit other families. This was so much fun since I got to play and learn new games while visiting other children. Each evening following the supper hour, Grandma would gather everyone for her evening devotion and prayer.

When I reached the age of seven, I was allowed to venture out on my own to walk to one of my cousin's homes to play. My cousin's family lived a few houses down the shoreline from my grandmother's home. There were no roads in Norway House back then, and everyone traveled by flat-bottomed boat or canoe. If one could not get a boat ride, he or she simply walked along the lake shore to his or her destination. The evenings were spent visiting people, the young folks listening to stories the older men told. I used to enjoy that very much. My cousins and I would often visit these old boys just to be entertained by their storytelling, and doing so soon became my favourite pastime. My favourite person was an old gentleman named Donald Houle. Donald ran a small candy store out of his home, and I guess that is why I enjoyed going to his place. We would munch on candies while listening to stories. Most of the stories were folklore or stories that taught a lesson.

One story I remember was about bears and how they lost their long, fluffy tails. One day, the bears set out to do some fishing on a lake near their home. When they arrived, they were surprised to see that the lake had frozen over the previous night; so they walked out onto the clear, thin

3

ice just to see if the ice was thick enough to support their weight. While they were on the lake, they were able to see fish swimming along the lake bottom, so they all sat down to watch. They were so interested in what was going on that they didn't realize they had sat there most of the day. When it was time to leave, they couldn't get up, as their warm tails had melted into the ice and the ice had refrozen. They tried several times to pull their tails out from different directions without success. Finally, the head bear suggested they help each other by pulling hard in hopes of releasing their tails. When they did this, the greater part of their tails was torn off, leaving them with a small stub for a tail. The following spring, their young were all born with short, stubby tails. So to this day, every bear has a short tail. I think the lesson here was to maintain your focus on your goals and to always mind your own business and not get sidetracked by what everyone else is doing.

The old gentlemen of the community would gather every night in someone's home, and we made sure we asked one of them during the daytime where he was going to meet that evening so we kids could come and join them. When these old men told stories of their past or someone's adventure, we would be so quiet that you could hear a pin drop. When it was time to go home for the night, we would discuss the stories we'd heard on our way home. I always hoped that my life would be as interesting as these old gentlemen's lives had been.

Mr. Joe Keeper from Norway House, Manitoba, was well known as a Canadian veteran, who had received a military medal for bravery, and an Olympian. I met him when I was a child during the summers we spent in Norway House. Later, during my teen years, I would see him walking to the Rossville United Church, and he would stop to talk to me. He knew my parents, and he often asked about them. Looking back now, I feel privileged for having met this man, for he instilled in me the desire to take on the challenges that allowed me to fulfill my dreams. He told me that we should never get discouraged when we fail to reach our goals the first time, for there will always be another opportunity. Mr. Keeper was best known for being a middle-distance runner. He set a Canadian record for running 10 miles (16.09 kilometres) in 54 minutes and 50 seconds in 1911 in Fort William, Ontario, before he was named to the Canadian Olympic team that went to the games in Stockholm, Sweden.

The Norway House community was located 456 kilometres (283.35 miles) north of Winnipeg, Manitoba, on the eastern channel of the Nelson River, about 30 kilometres (18.64 miles) north of Lake Winnipeg. The Nelson River and the Jack River flowed through the community, which was located on the shores of Playgreen Lake. These waters provided the early fur traders with many natural passages between the community of Norway House and other communities. My family and I travelled by canoe to Norway House from our home at Oxford House using these same natural water passages along the Nelson and Hayes River systems. My father used these water passages to transport his supplies for his trading post in Oxford House, Manitoba.

The Hudson's Bay Company built a trading post in Norway House on crown land, mainly for the fur trade, in 1814. The post was established on an island, which became known as Fort Island. The Archway Warehouse, jail, and the remains of the powder magazine can still be seen today. The Hudson's Bay Company hired craftsmen from the country of Norway to build the fort (1840–1841). Norway House community was named in these Norwegians' honour.

Missionary James Evans built the original Methodist church building on the Norway House Indian reservation in 1840. My parents were married in this church, and this was where my grandparents and their family worshipped. My parents and I attended this church during the summers we visited my grandmother. The church burnt down and was rebuilt on the same location in 1932. A new church building has now been erected behind the old church building, replacing it as the main sanctuary. The original church building is being kept as a historic structure. Evans is credited with creating the "syllabics" writing system in the Cree language in 1840 with the help of the Norway House Cree. As a young girl, my mother was taught to use the syllabics system, and she used it to communicate with her family by mail. The church hymnals had both the Cree syllabics and the English language.

Many things were happening in the world when I arrived on this earth in 1944. The Second World War was raging in Europe. Winston Churchill was the prime minster of Britain. The thirty-second American president was Franklin D. Roosevelt. The prime minister of Canada was Mackenzie King, and the premier of Manitoba was Stuart Garson, who also acted as the provincial treasurer. The Norway House Rossville reserve chief was Jacob Menow.

The war had taken its toll on everyone; many of the men who had left to fight in the war were reported missing in action or were killed. My father had to ration sugar and other products in his store because of our government's regulations and the shortages the country was experiencing. This was especially hard for Dad; he didn't like the idea of rationing since it would cause hardship for many of his customers. The families that trapped fur-bearing animals for a living purchased their goods once during the fall to last them all winter on their traplines—land areas set aside by the government to permit licensed trappers to harvest fur-bearing animals. Good news was hard to come by, and any news on the positive side was always appreciated. My parents would listen to the CBC news at noon every day to hear world news.

That fall, one piece of news was well received. History was made when an American aviator, Ann B. Baumgartner, became the first woman to fly a United States Army Air Force jet plane when she conducted an evaluation flight on the turbo-jet powered Bell YP-59A on October 14, 1944. She was the assistant operations officer in the fighter test section as a member of the Women Air Force Service Pilots program. Every woman must have felt proud upon hearing that news. The other good news was that the Manitoba government announced a record surplus during the summer of 1944.

So it seemed I was not the only blessing that summer. Considering all that was happening in this world, I am sure the highlight of my parent's lives was my coming into this world during that summer. I like to think that maybe all the hardships so many were facing were forgotten for a little while and that my arrival brought a little joy into my family's lives when I became the seventh and youngest child of our family.

Mor—A police officer and another man talking to a trapper.

The original Norway House United Church Building in Norway House, Manitoba.

The MS Keenora now sits in a museum in Selkirk, Manitoba.

Hudson's Bay Post in earlier days on Fort Island in Norway House, Manitoba.

Hudson's Bay Post at Norway House, Manitoba. A York boat is anchored off shore.

The MS Keenora *stopping at a lake port on Lake Winnipeg.*

One of many of Hyers Trading Posts.

Chapter 2
My Father

I T SEEMED THAT I was always getting into trouble when I went into my father's shop. I couldn't keep my hands off his tools, and I knew he took great care ensuring that each tool was cleaned, sharpened, and put back in its storage location. If he couldn't find something, he would call for me and ask if I had taken any tools from his shop. I would have to confess that I had played with the tool he was looking for; usually, I had left it where I had been playing. I didn't know then why he would get angry with me for misplacing or losing his tools. When I think back now, I realize he had to order the tools from the south and they probably took weeks or months to arrive, not to mention the cost, as we were located in an isolated community. I remember once, when my brothers were helping my father repair his motor toboggan (a snowmobile that looked like a toboggan from a distance, which was powered by a two-cylinder Indian motorcycle, air-cooled engine with a three-speed transmission) in the shop, I picked up the large pry bar they had been using, as I thought it would make a good spear. As I started walking towards the door, Dad saw me and called after me to drop it.

It just so happened that I was walking past a set of batteries Dad and my brothers had removed from the machine they were working on, and as I let the bar go, it landed on the batteries, contacting both battery posts. I became scared when the batteries started hissing and sparking and caught fire. When my father saw what was happening, he immediately removed the bar and assisted me out the shop door. I think I only touched the floor twice on my way to the door on the far end of the building. I don't know if I did much damage to the batteries, but he had the machine running again the following morning.

Dad must have been very forgiving and had a lot of patience with me. He continued to show his love for me and would spend a lot of time with me; he would take me with him when he went across the lake to the post office or to visit his friends, and I got to ride is his snow machine, which was always a thrill. Years later, he would take my brothers and me on his hunting trips, and I will always remember the good times we had just talking and sitting around the campfire after a good meal he had cooked. Sometimes, my brothers and I would sit and talk long after my dad had gone to sleep. Those were good times.

My father was a businessman who traveled a lot as a fur trader, and he would often grow a beard while he was on the road. As a small child, I would not recognize him with all this hair on his face and would be afraid of him. He started his career in the fur-trading business as a member of the Hyers Trading Company at Norway House when he was about eighteen years old. While there, he met my mother. They got married in 1926. Like many women in those early days, Mom was married before her twentieth birthday. After several years of training, the company transferred Dad to Gods Lake Narrows, Manitoba, as manager of that trading post; then a few years later, he was transferred to Oxford House to manage that post. While he was at the post in Oxford House, the investors of Hyers Trading decided to dismantle the company because they had reached retirement age. Dad acquired the property and the trading post at Oxford House, where he made his home. He expanded the business to include a sawmill. He also manufactured dog-team toboggans, cabinets, and sleighs built on runners that the trappers who travelled on the lakes used during early spring; he also repaired and recovered canvas canoes. I heard many stories about my father from many of the elders living in the northern communities of Island Lake, Gods Lake, and Norway House. Many of these elders were trappers when my father was a fur trader, and they told me he was fair in his dealings with them and he was known as someone who could be trusted. Hearing these stories made me very proud of my father.

The trappers my father traded with were local people who trapped and prepared the fur to trade for supplies in his store or sell for cash payment. Many trappers brought their furs to trade at my father's store and then established a cash account at the store to be used as needed. The trappers would then draw from this account during the summer months to make purchases from the store when they were not trapping, so the store was also like a bank for the trappers. The trappers would build a cabin on their traplines, and many of them lived in the cabins with their families. The trappers would train their children on the art of trapping—a skill that required much training to acquire. These young people could train and trap under their fathers' licenses. When the young trappers became adults at the age of twenty-one, they could apply to the provincial government for their own trapline and a license to trap. The trappers monitored the fur-bearing animals, moving their traps to different areas on the traplines so that the animals would continue to populate and they could be harvested again the following year. Some of these trappers worked for my father during the summer months at the sawmill or preparing our firewood for the following winter.

The fur trade was a very competitive business. As an example, Hyers Company built the first store on Rossville reserve. Shortly thereafter, the Hudson's Bay Company moved onto the reserve and built their store about 150 meters (500 feet) away from Hyers's store. It didn't take long before two independents built their stores between Hyers and the Hudson's Bay store, thus establishing four stores in a row selling the same products. So I am guessing that the store that offered the highest prices for the trapper's fur or carried the most products the trappers needed got the business.

As another example of the fierce competition in the fur trade, my father used to travel to the traplines to buy fur and bring supplies to the trappers. One season, a competitor (Northwest Company fur trader) left one day ahead of my father after learning of my father's itinerary. My father's plan was to meet the trappers in a north-eastern Manitoba community for the purpose of buying their furs. The competitor had stopped and camped for the night along the trail, while my father continued traveling late into the night, overtaking and passing him, thus gaining the distance he needed to arrive at the trappers' community for the fur purchases. When the competitor arrived at that community, he learned that my father had been there and gotten all the fur.

Abraham, an elder from the Island Lake area, mentioned that my father had a good dog team, with the endurance to travel long distances; others only wished their teams had as much endurance. (Later when I was an adult, the elders in Island Lake area told me that my father always offered the most for their furs. Therefore, they saved their fur to trade with him.)

When I was seven years old, the two best dogs from his team were still in his possession. The leader was well advanced in age, but the second dog was much younger. My father treated the dogs well, to the point of cooking hot meals for them. I used to watch him cooking fish stew or meat stew on the stove in his shop. He loved these dogs, and it was evident in the way he cared for them. I remember going with him to feed the dogs, and they would fuss over him. Even at a young age, I could tell he loved and enjoyed them.

I don't know where my father was born; I only know that he was an orphan and was adopted by an English missionary family. I never bothered to ask him, as I thought it would be rude to remind him that he was an orphan. He had a picture of his adoptive father sitting on a saddled horse. I am sure he had other pictures of his dad, as he had many pictures he had taken with a camera that looked like a small accordion. I always felt badly that he was orphaned and often wondered if his parents had given him up or died from some illness. I didn't want to ask him, fearing the risk of hurting him. It was something he would have to live with all of his life.

Later on, when I was nineteen years old, Dad and I travelled together in my car throughout Manitoba for the purpose of seeing the towns he had lived in while growing up. We visited the towns where his adoptive father had held pastoral positions in small country churches. Most of the buildings my dad had hoped to see again were now gone. He would reminisce about the many good experiences he'd had while living under his adoptive father's care. I could tell he missed those early days of his childhood—his emotions would become evident as he spoke of the good relationship he'd had with his adoptive parents. Still I could not get up the courage to ask him why he had been adopted since I feared that doing so might bring on bad memories. That trip was one of the many we would have together.

Sometimes, Dad would hear of my plans to travel to Winnipeg to see a dentist, and he would immediately inform me that he was coming with me. As we went about our business in Winnipeg, he would visit many of the professionals at their places of business and some elderly people who he called brothers and sisters in their homes. I didn't know then that these people were from the same orphanage he had come from.

During the summer months, my father would store his freight that arrived by boat from Winnipeg at his warehouse in Norway House. He personally built that warehouse to store freight for his Oxford House post. The freight consisted of household goods, such as canned foods, sewing supplies, clothing, and linens. This freight would be transported to Oxford House by canoe trains. These canoe trains made two trips to Oxford House every summer.

During the winter months, merchandise that was sold in my father's store was delivered by tractor trains form Ilford, Manitoba, where it was received and stored by the transport companies who owned the tractor trains. That freight would arrive at Ilford from Winnipeg on trains that the Canadian National Railway owned. The tractor train sleighs would be loaded with this freight and hauled to Oxford House once the ice on the lakes and muskegs was thick enough to travel on. I remember watching the men unload sleighs packed with various sized bags of flour that the local community would purchase to make bannock and bread. Because there was so much flour, it would take up most of the room in our large cold-storage warehouse.

The tractor trains were used to haul the much-needed freight annually for the stores in the isolated northern communities. The Caterpillar, or the International Harvester crawler, tractors were used to pull four large sleighs, each loaded with fourteen tons of freight. I am guessing the sleighs were about 5.5 meters (18 feet) long and 2.5 meters (8 feet) wide. The tractor trains had cabooses where the crews could eat and sleep since these machines travelled twenty-four hours per day. They also had fuel-tanker sleighs for fuelling their tractors, as there was no fuel station along the way. The tractor trains also hauled the year's supply of fuel for the hydro generators that powered the medical center and schools. The tractor trains hauled large materials like mechanical equipment, materials for housing construction, large hydro generators, boats, and canoes. Because this material could only be transported during the winter months since there were no roads into these communities, the train operators wasted no time getting all the material delivered. The transport companies also had competitors, which would take the jobs the following winter if they failed to complete their contracts. These tractor-train companies were privately owned by individuals who would sign a contract to deliver a certain amount of material and freight during the winter season. The mining companies and the fisheries also signed contracts with these individuals to haul their materials.

Tractor trains hauled our fuel for the wood stoves to our home. The tractor trains made two trips, hauling approximately 50 cords of wood that would last a year heating all the buildings. My dad's employees camped at the wood-cutting site to cut and prepare the wood during the summer months. After the wood was delivered to our property, I'd watch one of Dad's employees splitting huge piles of wood for the smaller stoves in our house. Once he completed the wood splitting, he would pile all the wood in neat, long rows to dry during the summer so it would be ready for use the following winter.

The mail plane arrived once a week at our community, and sometimes I would go with my brother, John, to meet the airplane at the Hudson's Bay Company dock, which was across the lake from our home. My father always received lots of mail, which the post office person would put into a mailbag that was made of canvas. John and I would wait for the mail to be sorted and then take the mailbag home. My father would unload the bag in our living room during the evening after supper. The mailbag's contents included lots of magazines, business letters, and mail from family and friends. Sometimes, we would receive a large parcel from a mail-order company. Dad would read and translate the letters from family and friends that were written in English. My mom would read to him if the letters were written in Cree syllabics.

A small plane called a Tiger Moth often arrived in our community. The Tiger Moth would haul a load of furs south for my father on its return flight. As a child, I had the opportunity to ride in one of these little airplanes. I was living my dream when I took that ride.

My dad personally prepared the shipment of fur pelts from the store; they would be counted and piled onto a burlap sheet and onto a press.

Another burlap sheet would be placed on top, covering the beaver pelts, after a correct number of pelts were piled. The wheel at the top was connected to a long worm gear screw and a flat plate, so when the wheel was turned, the press would compress the fur pelts and the two burlap sheets would come together so the edges could be sewn together with twine. The pressure on the press was then released, and the furs were now in tight 50- to 75-pound (22.68- to 34.02-kilogram) bales ready for shipment. Most of the fur being shipped south was compressed and wrapped in this manner. The fur was shipped to Winnipeg to a fur exchange for buyers to bid on and purchase for their companies. The only competitors my father had were the Hudson's Bay Company and the Northwest Company.

Looking back on my early childhood memories in Oxford House, I can't help but wish that every child could be as carefree and happy as I was. My parents were very special, and they valued the times the family came together. In the summer months, my father would take our family out on Oxford Lake in his big wooden boat that was capable of operating in rough lake waters. Some weekends, when it wasn't raining, we would spend our time on an island that was loaded with wild berries. My parents were always searching for new areas for berry picking. They were always finding that special area where berries were plentiful. We would pick tubs full of raspberries or blueberries to be canned and stored along with the rest of our winter food. We would take time out for fishing; swimming; and of course, picnics on the beautiful shores of Oxford Lake. I loved eating the fresh pickerel that Dad caught within the hour before lunch. I also enjoyed the nights we camped, when I could stay up a little later than usual and listen to my parents and brothers talking by the campfire and enjoy the fresh berries I was given for a late snack. Sometimes we would cross paths with other families along the way, and that gave me the opportunity to play with their kids.

My father had two large gardens that yielded potatoes and various other vegetables. The crop from the gardens would last us throughout the winter months, as these types of vegetables were not hauled into our community during the winter. We stored the potatoes in a large root cellar, which measured about 6 meters (19 feet) wide, 6 meters long, and 2 meters (6 feet) in height and was located under the floor of our house. This root cellar had a wooden floor and wooden walls, and was made up of two rooms, one for potatoes and one for canned goods. Shelves lined three walls of the room for canned goods, from floor to ceiling. My mother canned the vegetables and berries so they would not spoil. She also canned the moose and caribou meat to be used during the winter season. By the end of the next summer, we would still have a small supply of canned goods that would last until the new crops were ready to be canned.

My father and my older brothers resupplied our icehouse during the early winter by cutting ice blocks from the lake in 60-centimeter (2-foot) squares. The ice blocks were covered in sawdust to prevent them from thawing during the summer months. The icehouse was always cool, and the ceiling was loaded with hanging geese and ducks that were harvested during the fall hunting; the birds would also be a part of our winter food.

The best part about going to the icehouse was watching my brothers chip ice and put it into pails to be used for making ice cream. Occasionally on a summer day, we would make ice cream as a family. We would use a manual ice cream maker, which consisted of a wooden bucket with a smaller can inside it. You cranked a handle on the outside of the bucket, and it would turn a paddle inside the can, which would churn a mixture of cream and sugar. The space between the wooden bucket and the can was filled with ice, on which salt was poured to lower the temperature of the ice so that, as the cream was churned, it would thicken and freeze. Everyone took turns cranking the ice-cream maker. I was too small and too slow for them to let me have a turn, so I just waited until the ice cream was ready, and I would be the first to the table with my spoon. We would all have a generous helping, and my mother and father would give me an additional portion from their bowls as they both knew how much I loved ice cream. I guess the reason we didn't have ice cream often was that it was a lot of work to make it.

We also used the ice blocks to keep our food cool and prevent it from spoiling in the kitchen icebox. The icebox was like a fridge, except it didn't run on electricity. It had a compartment on the top that held a block of ice, keeping the rest of the icebox cool. A pan in the bottom compartment caught the water from the melting ice. The water from the melting ice was directed into a pipe then down into the catch pan below, and this water had to be emptied daily. The middle compartment was cooled by the ice, and that's where our food was kept.

During the summer, my family would make many trips out on the lake that lasted several days. These were multipurpose trips. Dad, with the help of my brothers, would set fishing nets to catch enough fish for my father's dog team's winter food and scout out new areas to harvest timber for my father's sawmill and firewood for our home, store, and my father's shop. The nets mostly caught whitefish, and Dad and my brothers would hang the fish on racks that stood 3.1 meters (10 feet) above ground by sticking a pole through the fish near their tails. About ten fish hung on each pole. The fish would dry on these racks and be left hanging until they were ready to be used for dog food during the winter months.

My father would often cook for his dogs in a large pot, making fish stew in his shop while he was making cabinets for newlyweds or some family that was moving to a larger house. The cooked fish stew would be enough to last a few days at a time. The fish stew included potatoes and other vegetables that he grew in his two large gardens. During the winter months, he often cooked meat the trappers gave him, and when the caribou came through in large herds, he would make caribou stew for his dog team. He would only cook for the dogs when he was home. When he would travel out on the trails, the dogs would simply get one or two frozen fish or a piece of frozen meat once a day, usually in the evening before they bedded down for the night. He quit using the dog teams after he purchased the motor toboggan.

My father spent a lot of time in his shop building canoes and sleighs or making dog harnesses to sell in his store. I avoided his shop when I knew he was building a coffin for someone in the village who had died. He felt it was an honour to be asked to make a coffin for someone in the community. He built the coffins to lighten the burden on the stricken families and not for any financial gain. It was the very last favour he could perform for a departed friend, and I always felt that he wanted to be alone during those times.

My father's fur-trading post was located on the same property as my parent's home at Oxford House, Manitoba. Our home was very comfortable, and it had an attached veranda that my father had built. Our family enjoyed that veranda during the cool summer evenings. The mosquitoes did not bother us since the open walls on the veranda where all screened off. The electrical power was supplied from our own powerhouse, which housed large glass batteries that were filled with liquid. Dad would run the generator once a week to recharge these batteries. This powerhouse supplied power to our house, our store, and the shop. The large warehouse was not connected to the electrical power system since there was no need for power there. Four other buildings did not need electrical power—the icehouse, the oil and gasoline storage building, the horse stable, and the marine house where the outboard motors and boating equipment was stored down by the dock.

I grew up with my father's hunting dog, Duke, who was a golden Labrador. My father would often take this dog with him for several days during the fall hunting season, when he and my brothers were hunting for geese and ducks. Duke loved the water, and when we were out walking together along the lake shore, he would bark, encouraging me to throw a stick out onto the water. He would immediately retrieve it then wait for the next throw. He never seemed to tire of this game. When we were swimming together, I would often hang onto him, and he would pull me along in the water. If I threw a rock into the water he would dive and bring up a rock that may not have been the same rock I threw in. I used to show him off to my friends, and they would be so impressed with the things Duke could do. He was my constant companion around our home area. I am sure he would have protected me if I was ever in danger—if, for example, we had met a bear or a wolf.

The only time other people got upset with this dog was during baseball games when he would run out onto the field, catch a flying ball, and run off with it. When he acquired one of these baseballs, he would either run home with it or bury it somewhere in the bushes. So I started leaving him home when I went to the games.

Duke had a habit of using his body to ram other dogs that came around our house. He would run full speed towards another large dog, and at the last second, he would jump up and sideways coming down hard against the side of the other dog and knocking it over. I am sure he surprised many dogs, as they were always preparing themselves for a head-on attack with teeth bared. The dogs that got rammed would get up, looking shocked; turn; and run home with their tails between their legs.

Sometimes, he'd surprise me by knocking me down. He'd ram himself against the back of my legs when I didn't think he was around. He would lick my face when he got me down, and I would laugh, as this tickled.

When my father took our family out camping on the lake, the wolves would howl during the night from across the lake, and Duke would bark at them with such volume that the echoes could be heard bouncing off the edge of the treeline on the lake shores. He had such a loud bark that, when I was near him, I would have to cover my ears. When I would tell him to be quiet, he would just look at me, tilt his head, and wag his tail as if to let me know he had it all under control. Finally, we would let him sleep in our tent just to keep him quiet so we could sleep.

My father's trading post at Oxford House, Manitoba.

Our home with the store in the background and the electricity-generating building on the right by the trees.

My brother John taking my nephew Bob and me for a dog sled ride.
My dad built the toboggan in his shop.

My nephew and I are playing with my father's two dogs from his dog
team. The dog on the right is the lead dog.

My father storing fur pelts in his warehouse.

Fur pelts being packaged for shipment.

My father sitting in front of his trading post.

Chapter 3
My Mother

MY MOTHER HAD A good sense of humour. She always made me laugh, especially when I was afraid. I always felt safe when I was with her, especially when she held me to reassure me that all was well. I was about five years old when we were returning home from a sport's day event on the other side of the lake. The wind was very strong that day, blowing in from the south. The waves on the lake were higher than dad's wooden boat. Mom and I were sitting near the front of the boat, and Dad was at the rear, operating the outboard motor. It seemed to me that our boat was tossed into the air each time we went over one of those big waves, and then it slid down the other side again into the valley of the waves. We were getting soaked from the water splashing over the front of the boat onto us as we ploughed through those big waves. My mother held me tight, knowing I was fearful, and she often smiled at me to reassure me. When we arrived at our dock, she turned to me and asked if I was all right. I simply nodded my head confirming I was okay, as I was cold from being wet. She said that the waves were so high and choppy that she was afraid a minnow would be tossed over the front of the boat straight into her mouth when she yawned and she wouldn't be able to spit it out against the strong wind. I laughed, as I thought that was funny.

My mother was born and grew up on the Norway House Cree Nation on a part of the reserve known as Rossville. I never met Grandma Nellie's husband, Grandpa Spence Poker, who had contacted tuberculosis (better known as TB). I learned years later that Grandpa Spence was shipped off to a TB sanatorium in Ninette, Manitoba, where he lived out the remaining days of his life. My mother never saw him again. Nor did she hear of his death at the time. He was buried at the sanatorium graveyard. Many northern people in those early days contracted TB, and I don't know if there was a cure then, as most of the people who were admitted as patients at the TB sanatoriums never returned home again.

Mom met and married my father in Norway House at the age of nineteen. It was normal for women then to be married before reaching the age of twenty. My grandma and mom's sisters used to tell me stories of how Mom and Dad did everything together and that Mom was always by his side when he had work to do, whether it was erecting a building or working in his shop. When I was a child, Mom and I would spend the evenings in his shop while she helped him with his work. They would laugh a lot as they shared their early childhood memories. It was a happy time for me since I got to play in the shop, and sometimes I could help Mom by holding parts for Dad as he assembled them. I watched these two people get along as a couple, and they really enjoyed being together. Mom often helped Dad pack furs for shipment since she didn't mind handling the raw fur. She was truly a perfect partner for him. During these wonderful experiences with my parents, I felt very happy to have been their child; these memories bring me great joy, and I cherish them and keep them alive in my heart.

Mom had several sisters and a brother, and they were a very close-knit family that expressed their excitement and love when they saw each other. I am sure the highlight of her life was going to Norway House every summer to visit with her relatives. I would sometimes get caught up in their excitement at seeing each other again. Many years later, I would go back to Rossville for a visit, and Mom's family would receive me with the same joy, excitement, and display of love that I'd experienced as a child. After visiting with Mother's family in Rossville, Mother and I would go back home to Oxford House, where there would be a lot of excitement at seeing our family and friends again. My father would travel with the canoe trains from Norway House that were transporting his freight, and he would arrive back in Oxford House a few days later.

After several days, the excitement of being home again would subside, and everything would return to the normal daily routine. My mother would sit at her favourite place outside overlooking the lake and in the shade of our house, probably remembering the good times she had experienced the weeks before in Norway House. She must have missed her mother, sisters, brother, and the friends she grew up with in Norway House. I would see her wiping the odd tear from her eye as I played on our lawn. When I would ask her if something was wrong, she would just say she was remembering happy thoughts.

I was twenty years old when my mother worked for the Clearwater Lake TB Sanatorium near The Pas, Manitoba, as a custodian. One day, I was approaching the front hospital parking lot to pick her up for the ride home at the end of her work day. It was a perfect day as far as the weather was concerned. One could hear the birds singing from every tree, and a gentle breeze blew over the lake, causing the leaves to make a rustling noise as they fluttered in the wind. I saw a commotion on the front hospital lawn where my mother was helping a nurse trying to comfort an Inuit woman who had attempted to leave the hospital. The Inuit woman had become homesick and attempted to run away from the sanatorium. My mother later told me that this Inuit woman was desperate and would have done anything to get back to the Arctic to see her loved ones again. It was obvious that this Inuit woman felt she was at the point of no return in her life, as she had given up all hope of getting back home again. She obviously didn't care if she died; she just wanted to be with her family again. The sanatorium's orderlies had captured her during her attempt to escape and had tried to get her back inside. The woman would not get up from the ground, where she sat crying.

No one in the sanatorium at that time spoke this woman's language. Even though my mother could not speak her language, she lovingly embraced the woman, who was crying her heart out like there was no tomorrow. I noticed that my mother was crying along with the woman, as she tried comforting her. Seeing that brought back memories of the many times my mother had lovingly held me like that as a child when I got hurt playing. I saw that old woman melt in my mother's arms, as she realized that here was another human being who shared her pain and cared for her.

In the days that followed, I would often see my mother and the Inuit woman sitting together, laughing at their attempts to communicate with one another. Over time, they were somehow able to understand each other, and my mother always visited the old woman on her days off, sometimes bringing her a sample of her home cooking. Seeing that Inuit women crying on the hospital lawn reminded me of how I felt when I was sent off to school at an early age and experienced homesickness in a strange land. As I watched, my emotions surfaced, and I found it hard to hold back the tears that attempted to gush out.

I will always remember my mother's show of compassion to a stranger who was sick and in need of a friend. My mother loved being around these sick people, and the thought of possibly contracting TB from them never bothered her. I often wondered if the memory of her father dying alone in a sanatorium like the one in which she worked drove her to help others overcome their loneliness. She offered them support in their hope that they might get back home someday.

My mother used to tell me stories about the birds and the animals and how they talked with one another. I always thought she was able to understand their communications. One morning, a bird was singing and chirping by my bedroom window, and she smiled and told me that the bird was laughing at me because I was still in my pyjamas well past breakfast. I took that very seriously and quickly got washed up and dressed. I didn't want that bird telling all the other birds that I'd woken up late that morning.

I enjoyed the stories she told me of the birds. Sometimes we would have lunch by the lake shore, and a seagull would pass by making a lot of noise squawking. She would tell me that that seagull was calling out to others that I had lunch and I probably wouldn't finish it, so there would be food for everyone. I didn't want the birds thinking I wasted my food, so I always made sure I cleaned up my plate. She also told me the seagull's job was to keep our lakes and shores clean, and that's why they were always patrolling the lake shores looking for messes that people left behind. I wasn't about to make a mess for them to have to clean up, so I always cleaned up after myself. The ravens patrolled the interior parts of the land away from the lakes. The birds worked well together to keep our planet clean.

My mother would plan our days so we could spend more time together, while my brothers who were home would be at the sawmill working or at my father's shop helping him repair machinery. My two older sisters, Rosie and Norma, were married and living elsewhere, and my youngest sister, Nellie, worked at my father's store. Sometimes, my mother would watch me swim and then we'd eat our lunch that she had prepared for us. It was times like this that I was able to show off my swimming skills to her. She never got tired of my entertainment, and she always seemed so impressed when I showed her how well I could swim or dive.

One day, I was swimming and showing off when I fell off a slippery rock I had been standing on in the water. The rock was in water so deep that, when I fell, I made a big splash but didn't fall on the rock. A loon on the lake and an arctic churn overhead started calling out and making a lot of noise. She told me the birds thought I was entertaining them and they were cheering for me. I felt very special hearing that, especially after being so clumsy and falling off the rock.

Mom grew up in a Christian home, and I remember as a child playing inside our home during those cold winter months, that I would stop and listen to her singing hymns in Cree. She had a Cree hymnal that she used to sing from during her personal devotion. She often sang those old hymns when she sat by my bedside in the evenings, and I would fall asleep happily listening to her singing. During the Christmas season, she would sing Christmas carols in Cree, and I enjoyed those very much.

My mother was a woman who kept to a schedule of her daily activities; laundry day was every Tuesday, no matter if it was cold, hot, or rainy. I remember one summer day the temperature must have been 30°C (86°F). She had moved her engine-driven washing machine outside for the wash day. Most people would have postponed their washing to a cooler day, but not Mom. I came home for lunch after swimming all morning, and the sun was very hot. One could see that she was very uncomfortable, as her face was beet red and she was perspiring. I asked her why she had to do laundry on such a hot day, and she told me she did laundry every Tuesday, and tomorrow there were other things she must do. It seemed she had each day planned, and the only thing that could change that was sickness, which she never had. She always told me that no tasks should ever run into the weekends, as those were for rest and family.

Mom had a smokehouse that my father built for her, where she could smoke fish that my brothers caught in fishing nets on Oxford Lake and sometimes fish the neighbours brought over to share from their bountiful harvests. She would let me know in advance if she planned to smoke fish or meat that day, and I would hang around the yard so I could help her in the smokehouse. She always started by showing me how to start a fire using birch bark and small kindling before adding the larger firewood. She would let me light the match that started the fire in the smokehouse firebox. I was always so amazed that a little flame from a little match could turn into a roaring fire. While we waited for the fire to make coals, she would hang the meat and fish on the upper level of the smokehouse. Once the fire got hot and there were plenty of red-hot coals, she would add willow sticks to the fire since these created a lot of smoke while they smouldered, causing the upper part of the smokehouse to thicken with smoke that would cure the fish or meat she was preparing. The upper part of the smokehouse had a small opening through which some of the smoke could escape. Mom explained that willow was her favourite wood for smoking fish or meat, as it added to the flavour of the smoked product. Later, she would spend much of the day adding more willow sticks to the fire and turning the fish and meat over so that it would be thoroughly cured. Some of this fish and meat would be put away for winter food. I always thought that it tasted good enough to be used for snacking between meals.

During the summer months, I would help my mom weed the gardens, and we would eat peas out of the fresh shells. Sometimes my nephews and my friends came over to help us, and they always told me they enjoyed helping us in our gardens. When we had enough for the day, my mother would pick some rhubarb to make pie, which was my favourite. Mom always gave the other kids some rhubarb to take home since we had lots of rhubarb plants that produced fresh new rhubarb stocks weekly. When fall came, everyone in my family helped to harvest the garden products. We would lay large canvas tarps out on our lawn so the potatoes could dry in the sunlight, as there was lots of moist dirt attached to these potatoes and the clay or dirt would fall away once they were washed and dried. My mother would direct my family as to where all these products went. The potatoes usually went into the potato bins in our basement. Some of the vegetables would be stored in the basement, while the majority would be canned for our winter food.

My mother was a very busy woman around our home; she did all the mending of our clothes since my two oldest sisters were gone, married, and raising their own families. The youngest sister, who was five years older than I, was away going to school down south. I would often see my mother up late making mitts, socks, and sweaters using woollen yarn. Some of these she would give away as Christmas presents. She would also make moccasins for everyone. Moccasins were shoes made out of moose hide that had flaps that went around the ankles tied with moose-hide laces. One year, she made me a pair of mukluks. The liners, made of rabbit fur, could be removed to dry or replaced with a clean dry pair.

My father and brothers had thick woollen pants they would wear when they were out at the lake getting timber for the sawmill or hunting caribou for fresh meat during the winter months. Mom would line these pants on the outside with canvas to make them strong, waterproof, and windproof. The woollen pants tended to catch on branches of trees and tear easily. She also made parkas insulated with goose-feather down to keep them warm in the minus-40-degree temperatures. I appreciated and enjoyed sleeping under the warm down quilt she made for me. She also made sleeping bags for my father and brothers using wild goose down; they used these during their fall hunting trips. She told me she'd made an extra thick sleeping bag for Dad when he used to travel with his dog team in the north, as he would sleep in a small tent along the trails at night.

One year, she made a fur parka and a fur pants for my dad as a gift, and he wore that outfit proudly over his clothes during extremely cold temperatures while riding his motor toboggan on the lake, going to a hunting area, or scouting timber for his sawmill. She used to make similar clothing for him when he travelled throughout the north using his dog team. He would rave about how warm he was when wearing the fur clothing that she had made for him. He would often express his appreciation to her. He was always doing special things for her like buying her little gifts she appreciated and needed. She would blush and say he shouldn't have done that, but I bet if he'd offered to return the gift, she would have refused to give it up. It was no wonder they loved each other so much, as they looked after each other like that.

My mother was full of knowledge when it came to finding a cure for a sickness or a remedy to heal an infection. I, and sometimes my nephews, would go with her when she went into the muskegs looking for herbs she used for remedies. She had knowledge of these remedies that her mother had passed onto her when she was a little girl. Being a child, I would pick up a common cold during the late fall or during the winter months. When my head was all plugged up, she would boil one of the roots in water then bring the steaming liquid into my bedroom, where the aroma would fill the room and give off an odour like Vicks VapoRub. This product would clear my head, unplug my stuffed nose, and make me feel like my cold was gone. I would sleep in total comfort throughout the night and be ready to play again the following morning.

Another time, she made a home remedy for a cut on my arm that had become infected. She crushed up a wild herb and applied it to my wound in a bandage. As soon as she applied the crushed herb onto my arm, I could feel the medicine drawing out and pulling the puss and infection from the wound on my arm. The next morning, the infection was gone; my open wound area had turned back to pink, and the puss was gone. Mom then made a salve to keep my open cut from drying, and it healed quickly. I was so impressed with the knowledge she had of traditional medicines. She had many of these remedies, which are now forgotten. She knew many other remedies for stomach aches, constipation, and fevers, and how to reduce swelling.

My mother enjoyed being outside anytime of the year. She used to have my brothers clean the snow off the lake to make a skating rink for us. During the evenings, she would take my nephews and me, and sometimes the neighbour kids, out for an evening of skating. My mother was a very good skater, and she would skate along with us. Most of us kids were just learning to skate, so she would teach us how to skate. At first she was always holding me up, as I was always falling down. But it didn't take long for me to learn, and soon we were all skating around the ice rink. I was glad she was the one who had taken the time to teach us to skate. My brothers wouldn't have had the patience to spend that much time with us kids every evening, when they could be out skating on the lake with their friends. Mom told me that they would skate for miles every evening along the lake shore, like all the older young people from our community. I am sure my mother also taught them to skate when they were small, but I don't remember asking her that.

During the winter, when we travelled across the lake on our snowmobile to attend church at the Oxford House United Church, she would hold me while I sat on the toolbox behind the rear seat since there were only two seats on the motor toboggan. I would watch the tracks the toboggan made as we travelled across the lake. Sometimes, we followed an old set of tracks, and I would be thrilled to see the ski-runner prints intertwining with the old prints. These prints in the snow looked alive as they moved back and forth over each other. They were two snakes performing a dance on the snow. I would face the rear of the snowmobile so the wind did not bother my face, as my mother always made sure I had my hood up and a big scarf tied around my neck and covering most of my face. I was one of those kids who always lost one mitten, so Mom would use yarn to connect them together up my sleeves and over my shoulders under my parka, and that way, they were always attached to me.

Chapter 4
My Sisters and Brothers

BEING THE YOUNGEST MEMBER of my family, I had three wonderful brothers who were my mentors and whom I loved and admired. I also had three of the most caring sisters, who were always looking out for my best interests. My sisters displayed our mother's qualities.

Rosie was my parent's first child. As a child, she went to the residential school at Norway House, Manitoba. She married Sam from Oxford House, and they lived about a city block from our house. Rosie and Sam were blessed with seventeen wonderful, healthy children, so I was never short of playmates. Her two oldest sons, Lawrence and Bobby, who were near my age, became my best friends and constant companions.

Rosie often came over to visit or just to see what our mom was doing, and she often helped Mom with chores around our house. I enjoyed being around Rosie, as she was a comfortable person to be around and she expressed her love by showing her concerns for me. I often thought that she was just like Mom, always there when I needed her.

Moving forward years later to 1988, we as a family had gathered to bury my father, who had died of natural causes at the age of eighty-one. Rosie saw that I was overcome with grief, so she came over to comfort me. She knew Mom was not able to comfort anyone at this time since she was also grieving my father's death. I realized that Rosie had the same qualities and attributes that my mother had, and that alone brought comfort to me. No wonder my mother always appreciated having Rosie near.

Norma was the second oldest child in our family; she was born a little over two years after Rosie. She also went to the residential school at Norway House. She married a railroad man, and they were blessed with six energetic, healthy children. She and her husband, Eric, lived in a railroad town along the Hudson Bay Railway line. The Hudson Bay Railway line ended at Churchill, Manitoba, on the Hudson Bay coast. Norma's family often came to visit us during the summer.

Ralph was my oldest brother and the third child born into our family. When he graduated from high school in Selkirk, Ralph immediately joined the Canadian Armed Forces, making the military his career. This career would take him to countries around the world that were in conflict. He was always away from home, so I didn't get to know him until I became an adult. As a child, I was very proud of him since my parents often told me what he was doing to protect our family's way of life and our country. My parents were very proud of him too, and they would often read and tell our family what he'd said in the letters he sent home.

George was the second male born into our family; and he came into the world a little over two years after Ralph. As a child, George also went to school in Selkirk, Manitoba. When he completed school, he was employed with the Canadian National Railway, which took him to various locations throughout Manitoba. He left home before I was born, but he would often come home to visit us for up to three weeks at a time, so it was then that I was able to get to know him.

I remember the countless hours he'd spend entertaining me by playing games with the toys he'd made or purchased for me when I was a child. He loved teaching me how to live and survive in the northern wilderness. He would take me hunting for wild chickens and show me how to shoot and hit the targets with his rifle. He was the very first person to show me how to trap and snare animals for food in the forest. He would always bring a lunch during our winter outings, and we would eat in front of a roaring fire he made. We would haul and pile extra wood beside the fire since he knew we would be there for a while. As we ate and talked, we would often stop talking and listen to the sounds of the wind as it blew through the large spruce trees around us. This was the same soft, gentle sound that used to put me to sleep when I was out camping with my parents. We would enjoy the warmth of the fire while listening to the sharp sounds of snapping and crackling as the fire consumed the wood. A wood-burning fire was so fascinating that your attention was drawn towards it, and you could lose all track of time as the flames danced and changed colour and the fire got hotter, and sometimes, it was as if the flames were doing a dance.

During the summer, George and I spent many hours playing with my toys outside, and sometimes, we would take a canoe during a hot summer day and travel to a nice, sandy beach to swim or go fishing at his favourite spot, where the fish were big and plentiful. He would cook the fresh pickerel fillet of fish that we caught, and he always brought extra spices; potatoes; bread; and of course, salt and pepper. George was a good cook, and the sizzling sounds of the fish cooking always made me hungry. Once the fish was cooked, we would take our first taste of the succulent fresh fish that melted in our mouths. We always ended up eating more than we should have, as it was that good.

When it was time for George to leave home for work, he would always come to me and ask what he should bring me the next time he came to visit. He sometimes reminded me of our dad, as both men enjoyed the company of others we met on the lake. George was always quick to offer our food, setting an extra place by our campfire; he was so considerate. He would tell me that he always found it hard to leave home, as he regarded my father as his best friend. I am sure he missed us all when he was away. He would often write to my parents, and he would occasionally mention my name in those letters, which made me feel appreciated.

John was the fifth child and the third male born into our family. He arrived twenty-one months after George had. John was eight years older than I, and he could always be found by my father's side when not going to school. He was always helping my father in the sawmill or in the shop. Unlike me, he was successfully obedient to my parents and the teachers at his school. John had a tender heart, and I could count on him as a brother who always looked out for me.

On one occasion, I was playing inside a friend's house when I noticed that it was getting dark outside. I suddenly realized my predicament—I was out later than I should have been—so I immediately went into panic mode. I put my coat and boots on and started running home in the dark.

I met John coming down the trail looking for me, and he warned me that my parents were starting to get concerned and advised me to prepare an explanation and an apology for them. We arrived home without incident, as I assumed they thought I was out walking with John, and he never said anything that would expose me since he knew my lateness was an oversight on my part.

John seemed to enjoy spending time with me, as he would often take me on canoe and dog-team rides. I remember the year he used me as a counterweight on a sailboard he built in our father's shop. The lake had just frozen over a few days prior, and the lake ice was still bare. The board had three skis, two of which were on one side along the main board. The sail was attached onto the main board where the operator sat. The outrigger ski extended far away from the main board, where he had me sit. When he raised the sail, the wind pushed us to record-breaking speeds out into the lake. I was so terrified I couldn't scream. In fact, I couldn't even pry my fingers off the ski to jump off. Each time he made a turn, the ski I was sitting on would rise about a meter (three feet) and then slam back down onto the ice. The rising and falling of the ski was continuous, and the height of the raised ski also terrified me. Once we arrived back home, he praised me for being so brave to withstand the high speeds we had experienced. I was only happy it was over, and I never went near the lake when he went sailboarding.

Nellie was my parent's sixth child, and the last girl to be born into our family. She was enrolled as a full-time student in a school down south, so the only time I saw her was when she came home during the summer holidays. She was only five and a half years older than me, and we always got along very well. It seemed obvious then that she was thrilled to have a little brother since she would fuss over me when she was home. We were siblings who enjoyed the same games and shared many funny stories that made us laugh.

We travelled together on my first trip away from home to a school in Selkirk. She was on her last year of school, while I was starting my first. She was my closest family member, friend, and companion when we both went south to school that fall. I don't think I could have survived without her during that first year away from home. We did not attend the same school, as she was in high school. Once she graduated, she went up north to work while I continued my schooling in Selkirk. She later met a handsome gospel singer, whom she married, and they were blessed with five good-looking and healthy children.

My father paid the expenses for four of his children to be educated in a southern school. His two oldest daughters, Rosie and Norma, attended the residential school at Norway House. John stayed at home helping our dad while attending a local school in Oxford House. My father's desire for those of us who went away to school was to receive an education in an English-speaking school and be exposed to different kinds of cultures.

Chapter 5
Oxford House, Manitoba

O NE BEAUTIFUL AFTERNOON, DARK clouds started rolling in from the south. The clouds were very low, and it appeared as if they could touch the tops of the trees. The gentle southern breeze was quickly turning into gusty winds from two directions; it churned the water into white-capped waves that became loud as they smashed against the rocky shoreline. My two nephews, Lawrence and Bobby, and I were swimming by my father's dock when we noticed the sun disappearing from overhead and the temperature dropping quickly. We quickly got out of the water and started getting dressed. We decided then that we would get some fishing lines and do some fishing off the dock instead. As we started fishing, we were catching the usual small northern pike that were plentiful in that area of the lake. We had planned to catch enough fish for Lawrence and Bobby's father's dog team, as we thought they needed fresh fish to eat.

Suddenly, the sky lit up with lightning flashes across the sky, and the sound of the thunder was very loud. When this happened, the fish went into a feeding frenzy, and we were catching larger pike. The water had turned almost black, and the waves were now very large. The tub that we had placed on the dock was quickly filling up with the fish that we caught. We decided to pull our lines out and go home, as we were getting soaked in the heavy downpour. Suddenly, I caught something that really tugged on my line, and I called out to my nephews to let them know I was struggling with a big one and I needed help to land it. When we saw the type of fish I had caught—a large lake trout—we all became very excited since we surely wouldn't give this fish to the dogs. We finally got the large trout onto the dock, and I removed my hook while my nephews held the fish still. It started flopping, and everyone let go of it as we were all afraid it would bite us if we tried to grab it. The fish flopped around the dock as we stood nearby watching, and suddenly it reached the edge of the dock and dropped out of sight into the dark lake water. At that moment it seemed that all time stood still, as our excitement disappeared with that lake trout.

We must have stood there for a while staring at the dark, cold water. I became aware that I was shaking from being cold, so we decided to take the tub of fish up and then go home for the day. This was a typical day for me while growing up at Oxford House, Manitoba, where each new day brought new adventures. I would always be grateful and consider it a blessing to have lived and grown up in this land of plenty that others only dream of.

The community of Oxford House is situated along the east side of Oxford Lake, which is on the Hayes River system. It is a First Nations Cree community and is referred to as Bunibonibee First Nation by the governing band council there. The main dialect spoken is Cree. Bunibonibee, which means "holes in the lake bottom," is the Cree name for Oxford House Lake. The Oxford House Lake water was very clean, and one could see about 4.5 meters (15 feet) below the surface; sometimes when I was walking along the rocky shores, I would see a fish swim by in search of food. When I was riding in the boat with my father, he would allow me to lean over the front of the boat as we were approaching the lake shore. Initially, I would not see anything but the darkness of the cold, deep water and the beams of sunlight dancing in the depth of the water like long snakes swimming and twisting their bodies as if trying to get away from our boat. Suddenly, the water would start getting lighter in colour, and I would begin to see the formations of rock boulders on the lake bottom like ghosts figures appearing out of nowhere. When I could see the lake bottom more clearly, the rocks looked like large grains of sand that were rising up gradually, which made me feel like we were descending from a height. I was always looking for a big fish, but we were always travelling too fast to see between the rocks.

Oxford House Lake produced large lake trout, walleye, northern pike, and whitefish, which were sometimes called "jumbos" because of their size.

The area was excellent for hunting; the caribou migrated to the area every winter, and plenty of moose lived in the area. The large timber growth was ideal for sawmilling and log-house building. The terrain around Oxford House was surrounded by hills, and some of the hills could be seen from a great distance. The lake shores were mostly bedrock, with the occasional sandy beach area. The community of Oxford House had two long beach areas ideal for swimming, as the sun warmed the shallow water in those areas to a comfortable level. The water level remained constant since there were no hydro dams on the Hayes River system to alter the water levels.

Years later, as an adult, I would work for the provincial government monitoring a heavy equipment training program during the summer. The training took place at the south end of Oxford House Lake along the winter road. (The winter roads were used during the winter months to haul supplies into the communities over frozen lakes and muskegs.) Most of the trainees were the trappers' sons from Oxford House.

One day, our supply airplane arrived with a passenger who represented the Caterpillar dealership from Thompson, Manitoba. He was sent to assist us with the equipment maintenance and parts inventory that we needed to keep on hand. It was about the fifth day when I noticed he was spending most of his time sitting alone in the camp kitchen, as he had completed most of the work he was sent to do. He was scheduled to depart on the next supply plane, which was two days away. Our supply airplane made weekly trips to our training site, weather permitting. I was planning to go to a nearby waterfall to do a little fishing, so I asked him if he wanted to come. He told me he did not fish and had never used a fishing rod.

He finally agreed to come along, with the intention of keeping me company. The lower area of the falls was well known for its large northern pike, weighing up to 18 kilograms (about 40 pounds). The falls were very loud, and the water was fast moving at the drop point, where the big fish usually fed. I immediately caught several large pike, and the Caterpillar representative seemed very impressed with my ability to catch fish. I asked him if he wanted to try, and again he refused. Finally, when I decided I had enough fish to take home, I again offered to teach him how to cast with the fishing rod. It took a bit of coaxing, but he finally agreed to practice and make a couple of casts into the water before we headed back to the camp. I put a lead weight at the end of my fishing line instead of a hook so he could practice casting on dry ground while I was cleaning the fish I had caught. It didn't take him long to learn, so I exchanged the lead weight for a fish hook. At first, he just stood there looking at the water flowing over the rock formation. I assumed he was awestruck by the sound and power of the waterfalls. He finally made his first cast, and no sooner had the hook touched the water than one of those large northern pikes grabbed his hook. At first, he looked so scared I thought he was going to drop my fishing rod into the water, but he hung on. The big fish was fighting mad, and I could see the representative was starting to enjoy the challenge. After he had caught a couple of large pike, he immediately released them back into the water.

As we walked back to the camp, he seemed very excited as he talked a mile a minute about the way the fish fought when he hauled them in. During supper that evening, he told everyone about the huge fish he had caught at the falls, and of course the group teased him by demanding to see his fish.

After we finished supper, he came over and asked if he could borrow my fishing rod again since he and one of the trainees wanted to go back to the falls to do some fishing. When I went to bed that night, I heard he was still fishing at the falls. The next morning at 6:00 a.m., I walked into the kitchen for breakfast and learned that our new fisherman had gotten up very early to go back fishing. He was truly hooked.

The supply airplane finally arrived, and he was happy to be going home. I asked him if all the parts we had ordered could be assembled and shipped back within two days. We could arrange for the airplane to bring those parts back to our camp, as they were badly needed. Sure enough, the airplane arrived, along with the parts and our new fisherman! He informed me that he had purchased his own fishing gear and was back to do more fishing.

I used to watch, with great interest, the mail airplane that arrived once a week during the summer and winter months. The only place this airplane could land was on the lakes, as there were no airstrips in the communities at that time. These bush planes were fitted with floats in the summer and skis during the winter, enabling them to land just about anywhere on the lakes and rivers. The weekly mail plane that brought the mail was a Bittern Norseman. It also hauled passengers from one community to another and south to Lac du Bonnet, which was the nearest sea base to Winnipeg. From Lac du Bonnet, one would travel by car into Winnipeg. Many of the trappers and their families used this air service to go south to a Winnipeg hospital or for medical appointments.

The community of Oxford House began as a supply depot for the Hudson's Bay Company's fur-trading posts from which to move supplies en route to Norway House. Originally, the aboriginal people from the surrounding area and from York Factory moved to the trading site. The Hudson's Bay Company hired many of these people as store clerks, while others got work on freighter canoes in the summer and as dog-team mushers during the winter months hauling supplies and fur. Oxford House officially became a community in 1798.

Fur trapping was the main source of income for the people of Oxford House. During the early 1950s, some of the families left the community to live on their traplines during the trapping season, which was during the winter months. Once the early winter trapping was done (usually by Christmas), the trappers would bring in their furs to the store to trade for supplies, and our warehouses would start filling up with piles of beaver pelts and muskrat, weasel, fox, fisher, mink, and other types of furs. Some of these furs would be hung from the ceilings, and you had to walk through them to get to the other end of the building. I used to love the feel of the soft fur on my face as I walked through them. We had one warehouse filled with so many furs that both ceilings on the two-story building were filled with hanging fur. These pelts would later be packaged for shipment south on chartered aircraft. The planes would haul the furs south in time for the fur auctions that were held in Winnipeg, Manitoba, during the spring.

The next time these trappers would arrive with their furs would be in the very late spring, when they travelled with their canoes on their sleighs. When traveling on the deteriorated ice in late spring, the dog sleigh would sometimes break through the ice, allowing the canoe to float and the furs being hauled in the canoe would be kept dry. The dogs could also be rescued by pulling them into the canoe, but usually they would be able to get each other out as they were harnessed together. When one dog got out onto good ice, that dog would pull the other dogs out. It was unusual for all the dogs to fall through the ice at the same time. Occasionally, the water currents under the ice deteriorated the ice more rapidly than the warm weather on the ice surface. Getting wet during the warm spring weather didn't bother these dogs, and they would shake the water off and keep going. The work of pulling the sleigh kept the dogs warm.

Sometimes, the trappers came back to the community very late in the spring, and the canoes would float on the slush water above the ice, or the trappers would manoeuvre around the floating ice; everyone, including the dogs, would remain in the canoe with the sleigh during the open water crossings. When they got to the end of the lake, to portage or move onto good ice, the canoe would be mounted on the sleigh once again and the dog team would pull the canoe on the sleigh along the portage to the next lake. This would continue until the team reached its destination. If it was an extremely warm spring and the snow had thawed out on the portage trails, the trapper would carry his canoe, furs, and materials to the next lake. The dogs would still pull the sleigh but with limited load since the bare ground made it hard pulling.

Arrival into the community was always the highlight of the journey, as these trappers would have the opportunity to see their families again. It was exciting to see the kids who'd stayed with their parents on the traplines. Their return was an annual event filled with excitement, as the trappers' kids would tell us about their exciting adventures on their traplines. We would listen with envy, especially when they told us how much money they earned by helping their dads harvest the animals on their traplines. I always dreamed that someday I would go out into the wild and spend the winters trapping.

As a child, I had the opportunity to observe and learn how to trap some of these animals. Charlie was a local trapper who used to take his son and me out into the forest near our community to learn how to set traps and study the habits of the fur-bearing animals. Charlie and his family were good friend of my parents, and he lived a short distance from our home. He would show us how to set traps for beavers, muskrats, squirrels, and rabbits. I used to lay awake at night, anxiously awaiting daylight to arrive so we could get out there to see what we'd caught. Learning the trapping skills was fun, and I enjoyed being with Charlie's family. His children were my good friends, as I'd spent many hours at their home playing baseball in their yard.

As a fur trader's son, I learned many things from my father about the fur trade. As an example, fur trapping is only done during the winter months when the fur is in its best condition and the fur is thickest. The fur got thicker during an unusually cold season, and this prime fur brought the most profit to the trappers and the traders. Our local trappers used baited traps along the animal's path that would attract the animals using food as bait. The snare wire noose was also a common method of trapping animals. After the trapper made his daily rounds checking all his traps, he would return to his cabin to start skinning the animals. Once the skins were removed, they would be stretched on wooden or wire drying frames, and then the fat and meat on the pelt would be scraped off before the trapper would hang them to dry. These drying racks usually hung near their wood stoves to dry overnight. Once the pelts were dry, the trappers would remove them from the frames and hang them for storage to prevent the mice from chewing on them. The beaver pelts were piled up together then rolled up into a round bundle.

I heard a story about the method used to manufacture beaver pelt hats. Apparently, a mixture that included mercury was used, probably to soften the skin. Mercury is poisonous, and the hat manufacturers breathed in these fumes while they worked on the hats, eventually going insane. This is where the saying "mad as a hatter" came from. This method was invented by the English in the early 1700s.

Trapping was a way of life for the majority of the people in our community, and it was a good livelihood for many. The meat from the trapped animals was shared for human consumption, and some would be canned and used during the summer months. The meat that was not desirable was used for dog food.

*Trapper travelling with his
dog team in late spring.*

Trapper hauling his canoe on a dog sled during spring thaw.

My father's new store building in Oxford House, Manitoba.

Our family home in Oxford House. The store building is the background and the electricity-generating building is on the right by the trees.

A York boat parked at Oxford House, Manitoba.

*My father's trading post building at
Oxford House, Manitoba.*

My father in front of the Hudson's Bay Post.

*My nephew Lawrence on the left standing with me
in front of the house.*

Chapter 6
The Toothache

OUR HOME WAS LOCATED on the shores of the beautiful Oxford House Lake on a point of land across from the nursing station, which was the only medical facility in the community. This was where I experienced my first tooth extraction at the age of five, when a visiting doctor was in town. I had been having trouble sleeping at night because of pain that had developed from a decayed tooth. The tooth decay was so advanced that the pain was almost unbearable, but I tried keeping it a secret from my family as long as I could. I was afraid if I told my parents they might take me to the nursing station, where I thought the head nurse would tear out my tooth and gums without mercy.

The head nurse at the nursing station would extract teeth between the doctor's visits. If more than a simple tooth extraction was required, a person was sent south to have a dentist make the repairs. The time between each doctor's visits could be months. I guess I was fortunate that a visiting doctor was in our community at the time.

My toothache pain would start during the night after everyone was asleep. Finally, one night, the pain was so great that I started to cry, so I got up to walk around my room holding my right cheek. I discovered that standing up seemed to lessen the pain, but I knew I couldn't do that all night. If I walked around in circles all night, my parents would know something was wrong, as I'd be sleepy in the morning.

My mother came into my room when she heard me getting out of bed around 10:00 p.m. and asked with a concerned look on her face, "Are you ill or is something bothering you?"

"I have a sore tooth that is getting worse daily," I said.

"Open your mouth, and let me see if I can see the cause of the pain," she said.

I opened my mouth to let her look.

"I can see why it's so painful," she said. "The decay has opened the top portion of your tooth." She held me the rest of that night until I fell asleep. Her hugs always brought a soothing comfort, but this time those hugs didn't have an effect since my tooth still hurt. She even tried using a store-bought item for toothaches, but it didn't seem to help. It was always after midnight by the time the pain went away; then I would fall asleep for the remainder of the night. By then, my tooth had been hurting for about a week.

Mom must have told my father the next morning because he was waiting for me at the dining room table when I got up. "Good morning, did you sleep well last night?" he asked.

"I slept so well that I slept in this morning," I replied, a little embarrassed at being seen getting up so late.

"You and I are going to the nursing station this morning after you have breakfast to see the visiting doctor, who we will ask to look at your sore tooth," he said.

"My toothache is gone now," I replied.

"Even so, I still think we should go and see him. I will be back to get you in one hour, and that will give you time to have your breakfast," he said as he got up to leave.

"He will be ready to go after a good breakfast," my mother said speaking up on my behalf.

And with that, Dad went out the door.

"You will be glad you went to see the doctor since he will fix your tooth and you will not have that toothache bothering you anymore. Then you will be able to have a good night's sleep every night thereafter," Mom said giving me a quick hug. "We better get your breakfast right away before your dad comes back," she added, as she walked towards the kitchen.

Now that my father knew about my toothache, I knew there would be no changing his mind, as I'd learned from experience that, once he made a decision, he followed through.

"Are we ready to go?" he asked, walking into the living room where Mom and I sat.

"He sure is, and he had a big breakfast this morning. He even ate two extra pieces of toast as well," Mom replied.

"That's good since we may be gone longer than I thought. I received word this morning that I need to stop at the school to talk to the teacher," he told Mom.

"I will keep lunch warm if you two are late," she replied. "Be a good boy, and don't be afraid of the doctor. He is only there to help make you better," she told me as we parted.

"I don't like going to the nursing station," I called back. "It always smells like medicine."

"Good-bye and hurry back and tell me all about your visit with the doctor," she called after me.

I had gone to the nursing station many times to get vaccinations for smallpox, polio, and diphtheria, just to name a few. I had also gone there to receive my supply of cod liver oil, which every child in our community had to take as part of a government health program to strengthen our immune systems. The nurse would make sure every child got their share, and it was up to the parents to make sure their children received the required daily intake. The older kids who were in the local schools would have to go to the nursing station to receive their daily portion from the nurse. My dad took me to see the doctor because I would not have gone to this house of medicine, which I was afraid of, with one of my brothers or sisters, and my mother did not speak English well enough to explain to the doctor what was wrong with me.

When we arrived at the nursing station, my dad immediately informed the doctor of my problem. Once the doctor understood my need, he had the nurse take me to a room that had a large wooden chair for me to sit on. The doctor came in and made hand movements that I didn't understand. The doctor called to my father, and when he came into the room, the doctor said something to him.

Dad looked directly into my eyes and put both his hands on my shoulders. "I do not understand why you are not listening and doing what this doctor says as we agreed you would do, remember?" he said in Cree, which was my mother tongue and the only language I spoke.

"I don't understand what he wants. He is waving his hands a lot but hasn't said what he wants me to do yet," I explained.

"He wants you to open your mouth so he can look at that tooth that is bothering you to make the necessary repairs," Dad explained.

"Oh," I said, and I immediately opened my mouth for the doctor to look at my sore tooth.

After the doctor examined the inside of my mouth, he talked with my dad, and I got to leave for a while to wait in the waiting room. My dad finally came out of the room where the doctor had looked at my tooth. "You were such a good boy allowing the doctor to look at that tooth," he began. He explained that the doctor had found the problem and that was good news. He told me the doctor would call me back in to repair the tooth and urged me to continue being brave and doing as the doctor instructed. "I am so proud of you!" he exclaimed. "I have to leave for a while to talk to the teacher at the school next door, but I will be back very soon to take you home. You just have to wait right here until I get back and remember to do as the doctor says, all right?

"The nurse knows that I have to leave you here for a while," he added, "and she agreed to look in on you once in awhile. She's going to get a nurse's aide who speaks Cree to help you talk to the doctor. And remember, I won't be long. So I will see you very soon, okay?"

I nodded my head and smiled at him in confidence; this sounded like the doctor was going to make my toothache go away. "Don't be too long," I replied. "I don't like being in this place."

With that, he smiled, waved good-bye, and left. I continued to sit in that waiting room watching other people taking their turns seeing the doctor. I didn't see any of these patients come charging out screaming with terrified looks on their faces, so things were going well and I was feeling more comfortable as my fear of the doctor and the nurse was starting to fade away.

As my father's youngest child, I was always determined to be an obedient son, and I always tried to please him as this made him very proud of me. There was nothing he couldn't do, and I knew he had confidence in me. I didn't know if my father sensed my fear of the doctor and the nurse, but inside I was terrified of them, which I tried to hide from them and my father.

Soon my name was called, and I went in and sat in the big chair so the doctor could look at my tooth again. The nurse's aide, who spoke Cree, translated what he said, and everything was going well. "The doctor is going to give you a shot beside your tooth that will take away the pain," she said, looking at me with pity. "So you need to open your mouth wide for him," she added.

The doctor had the syringe in his hand, but I still didn't move. I kept my mouth open, remembering my father's departing words—*I am so proud of you*. With that in my thoughts, I was willing to put up with the pain of getting that shot. The doctor must have been very impressed with me after I let him stick that syringe into my mouth, which I didn't end up minding since the shot didn't hurt as much as I'd thought it would. *After all*, I thought, *what pain could a little old syringe bring?* I'd had a few shots on my arms and rear cheeks, and they hadn't hurt that much. I was getting used to them anyway. I was often getting some kind of vaccination to prevent me from catching some sickness.

Once the doctor finished giving me the shot, he left the room, and I continued sitting there with my mouth wide open.

The nurse's aide came back a minute later and said, "You can close your mouth for now. We will be back in a little while."

While sitting there, I began to notice a strange feeling developing on the right side of my face.

When the doctor returned, he talked to the nurse's aide, who then asked, "Are you feeling anything out of the ordinary on your right cheek?"

"Yes," I replied, "it feels like my cheek is growing very big, and I can hardly feel when I touch it."

She said, "That is what the doctor wanted to hear. The anaesthetic is supposed to take the feeling away; it is called freezing."

I became alarmed when I heard that. "I don't want a frozen cheek," I said, imagining that my skin would turn dark and puffy and start to peel off. "Is my cheek turning white now from being frozen?" I asked her.

She must have noticed the alarm in my voice. "This is a different type of freezing," she explained. "It's not like freezing your cheek outside in the winter. With this type of freezing, your cheek will return to normal in a couple of hours, and you will not notice anything different."

I was kind of relieved to hear that, but now I was concerned as to what else might happen.

The doctor picked up a tool that looked like a pair of pliers. I wasn't having that put into my mouth, so I shut my mouth tight. After all, I didn't know what he was going to clamp onto once he got that tool in my mouth. I would not open up for them. They finally gave up trying. I was told to go back to the waiting room. "The doctor is going to tell your father that you would not cooperate unless you come back in here and open your mouth so the doctor can finish his work," said the nurse's aide with a threatening tone in her voice.

I didn't say anything in reply, as I had no desire to go back in there. Besides, now I was really scared of the doctor and what my dad might say. Her last statement scared me as I was often told when caught doing something wrong that my dad would hear about this, and I never wanted my dad to be displeased with me. I felt I was hurting him when I disappointed him. I always wanted to be obedient to my parents.

When my dad arrived, it was obvious that he was very disappointed with me for not cooperating with the doctor. "We are going back into that room so the doctor can finish fixing your tooth," he said with a disappointed look on his face. "I don't understand why you didn't listen and do as the doctor instructed," he added, a questioning look crossing his face.

So we went back in. I suppose Dad thought his presence in the room would reassure me so that I would yield.

Again, I refused to open my mouth as long as the doctor had those pliers in his hand. I had seen my father and brothers using pliers on the machines they worked on, and sometimes they grabbed the gaskets or seals and tore them out piece by piece. I had visions of the doctor doing the same to my mouth. They tried holding me down, and they tried to pry my mouth open, but I would not open.

They finally gave up, and we went home. My father was very disappointed. He said very little on our way home.

I was again up half the night with the toothache, and my mother sat up with me feeling sorry for me. "Why didn't you let the doctor remove that decayed tooth?" she asked.

"I was afraid the doctor was going to hurt me," I said, starting to cry.

"Now your dad is very disappointed with you, and he feels he has failed you somehow. So now you are going to have to do that all over again tomorrow. I am afraid that your dad may get angry with you, and it may hurt you more if they have to force your mouth open to pull that tooth out," she said almost crying, and I could see she was very concerned. "We love you very much and only want the best for you. The only reason your dad is working late tonight is he knows that he will not sleep much because he is worried about you and the pain you are having to experience," she added with great concern. "You could have slept well tonight and felt good tomorrow if that tooth was gone, and it would have been all over with by now."

I started to feel very sorry and angry with myself for not letting the doctor pull my tooth and especially for disappointing my father. I told her this, trying my best not to cry.

The following morning after breakfast, my father was sitting in the dining room having his morning tea with Mom. "We are going back to the nursing station this morning, and I am going to stay and help the doctor remove your decayed tooth. Remember, *we are going to remove that tooth!*" he said. He voice sounded deep, and he had a determined look on his face.

"I will try to cooperate, and I am sorry that I caused you so much grief," I admitted.

My mother held my hand until it was time to leave. Then she said, "I know you will cooperate with your dad and the doctor today, so when you come home, I will make your favourite, rice pudding." Everyone in my family knew that her rice pudding was my favourite dessert. "And I know you will be able to sleep soundly tonight with that toothache gone," she called as I left.

When we arrived at the nursing station, we didn't have to wait very long before the same nurse's aide called my name. My father and I both walked in the doctor's room. "Remember, we are going to remove that decayed tooth today," he said, as I sat down in the same big, wooden chair.

I didn't say anything; I was now trembling from fear, and I felt very weak. I saw the same type of syringe sitting on a table behind the doctor, who stood there looking out the window. Once the doctor got started, I cooperated to the same point I had the previous day. I felt the freezing take effect. But when it was time for the pliers to be used, I shut my mouth tight again and would not open up for them, as I was becoming very fearful that the doctor was going to do damage to my mouth and cheek. "He's going to hurt me with those pliers," I called out to my father, as they struggled with me, trying to open my mouth.

The three of them fought with me, but I still wouldn't open my mouth since I was so scared my mouth would be torn apart by the doctor's pliers. They finally gave up, again.

"Stay here and rest while I go out and talk to the doctor," my father said.

My father, the nurse's aide, and the doctor went out of the room leaving me there wondering what would happen next and relieved the pliers hadn't gone into my mouth. By this time, I was feeling good about my success in having prevented the doctor's efforts to open my mouth and tear my mouth apart. I knew now that I had the power to prevent that from happening, and I was no longer scared. *Maybe my dad will talk the doctor out of using those pliers*, I thought, feeling much better and still having confidence in my father's wisdom to help me. Yes, this was beginning to make my day, and I was actually starting to feel good about things. Now I was more determined than ever not to let that doctor use his pliers to tear my mouth apart.

My dad and the doctor finally returned from their talk, and I was hoping my dad had talked some sense into the doctor. "Open your mouth for the doctor," my father said.

"I will not open my mouth for the doctor to tear my mouth apart with those pliers," I said, starting to cry, for the fear was growing in me again.

The doctor then showed me another device he had in his hand, and he pointed to the cotton covered areas. "The doctor wants you to just bite on the cotton-covered tips to check the strength of your bite," the nurse's aide said.

This sounded all right to me, as I was puffed up with the pride over my success in overcoming their attempts to open my mouth. After all, I didn't see anything wrong with showing off my powerful bite. *Maybe the doctor has finally smartened up and will try something else to repair my tooth*, I thought. "All right, I can do that," I said confidently to the nurse's aide.

So I opened my mouth. The doctor put that device into my mouth onto both of my front upper and lower teeth. I clamped down hard on those soft cotton ends, and suddenly, that device snapped open, causing my mouth to open wide! I could hear the crackling of my jaw muscles as they were being stretched to the limit. My dad and the nurse quickly grabbed and held my arms down, while my father wrapped his other powerful arm around my head so that I could not move. The doctor grabbed his pliers, and the next thing I heard and felt was the breaking loose of my sore tooth from my jaw. Then I felt my blood running down into the back of my throat, and this sudden change of circumstances sent me into a state of shock so that I couldn't move after they released me.

The nurse's aide held a pan in front of my face, so I spit my blood into that pan while she wiped the blood and saliva from my mouth. I noticed that I couldn't feel the tissue on my cheek and mouth when she wiped that area, and I suddenly had a horrific thought—my cheek and mouth had been torn off! I jumped off that chair and literally ran towards the mirror on the wall to look at my mouth through my tear-filled eyes. I was utterly relieved to see that everything was still there, and then I remembered that it was the freezing that deadened my senses on my cheek and mouth.

The doctor and his aide showed me the extracted tooth, which was badly decayed.

With that over with, my father and I went home, and I cried like a baby all the way. On the boat ride home, I was sure I saw a smile of satisfaction on my dad's face. *After all, he always succeeds in overcoming every obstacle that stands in his way*, I thought.

When we got home, my mom had my rice pudding sitting by the stove waiting for me. I was going to enjoy that rice pudding for the next few days, and it was all just for me! That night, I slept well, as I had only my hurt pride to nurse back to health. My mouth healed after many rinses with a warm water and salt solution my mom prepared for me. My relationship with my father improved, as now I knew I could always trust him, knowing that whatever he wanted me to do, it was always for my good.

I always loved, admired, and respected my father, and this was one of those foolish childhood incidents where I failed to trust him; I actually thought that he didn't recognize that the doctor didn't know what he was doing! I also didn't believe that he knew what was going to happen when that doctor pulled out those pliers. I thought I knew better and could see more clearly. We talked about this, and I told him that my faith in him had failed the moment when I saw those pliers, thinking that he had sided with the doctor. I apologised and expressed my shame for not trusting him. He told me that he thought I was just being stubborn and afraid. He was right about me being scared, and I saw that yielding to my fear had led me astray. I knew that he would have never let anyone hurt me. I believe to this day that he would have laid down his life defending me. I felt badly that my faith in him had failed me since he was an honest person and a respected businessman, whose customers trusted and liked him. Our relationship as father and son grew, and it was based on trust and respect.

Chapter 7
Foolish Incidents

T HE COMMUNITY OF OXFORD House, Manitoba, was located along the historic Hayes River, once travelled by fur traders en route to Hudson Bay. The community sat on the eastern shoreline of Oxford House Lake. During the early fur trade, the trade goods flowed through Oxford House in the Hudson's Bay Company's York boats. As a child, I would travel with my family in canoes, as my father used these same routes along the Hayes River system to resupply his trading post in Oxford House annually. Some of the local people in those areas still use these routes today to travel from one community to another. The settlement of Oxford House originated as a Hudson's Bay Post about halfway between York Factory and Norway House, Manitoba.

Our home was located on a peninsula along the eastern side of Oxford Lake. The high elevation levels of the land where our house, store, and generator buildings were located overlooked the lake on three sides. The area around the lake was hilly, and one could see for miles on a clear day, especially when looking towards the west, where other large hills and lakes could be seen. Part of the north shore on this point had a sheer rock face where the local young people often came to swim and dive off the rocks. The lake bottom had a steep downslope descending from the shore into the lake so it was very deep near this shore. Lawrence and Bobby and I would often play in this area, just a bit west of the sheer rock face. The smooth, flat rock shoreline there descended sharply, starting from above the water and travelling down through the water, where it continued to descend at a steep angle deep into the lake. We would slide down the wet slippery slopes of these rocks. We either stood or sat while sliding down into the water until we hit the water and it went over our heads. There would be a lot of shouting and laughing as we watched each other's antics. Another favourite area off this north shore was a small rock island that we could walk to. We'd spend a good part of many days swimming. The water level between it and the main shore was only about a meter (3 feet) at the deepest. The shallow bottom had fine sand like that at a beach paradise, and the water was always warm from the sun. The opposite side of the island had a steep drop-off point into an area of small boulders about 30 centimetres (12 inches) in diameter, and the water there was always cold.

My father's sawmill, shop, warehouses, dock, and a marine building where he stored his outboard motors, canoes, and other boating equipment stood on the peninsula's eastern shore. On the shallow bay off this shore, you could see the colour of the water change over the white, sandy bottom of the lake. The shoreline along this bay was mostly white sand beach with a small river draining into the lake from the inland muskegs. The shoreline area at the discharge end of the river had a marsh growth, with lily pads that provided shelter for the smaller fish. The Catholic Mission dock was also located in this bay, and you could see the mission buildings and their electrical windmill generator tower over the treetops from our house.

The peninsula's western shore was mostly solid rock with an occasional small beach. The lake bottom towards the west and north was a mixture of sand and rock boulders. My father had his oil and gasoline storage building up the hill in this area behind the store. The oil and gasoline was stored in sealed 205-liter (45-gallon) drums. The icehouse was farther south along the shore, down the hill from our house. The gradual slope into the lake at the beach area was used to haul ice during the winter months to resupply the icehouse. This was also the area where our firewood was cut, chopped, piled, and seasoned.

I was about seven years old when I had gone swimming alone in an area that I would not normally be found swimming. I was there because I'd seen the older boys diving off the high rocks along this rocky shoreline the day before. As I'd watched these young men diving, I could see from their facial expressions and the sound of their laughter that they were really enjoying the thrill of high diving. They were shouting to one another with challenges to do better than the last diver. They were having a great deal of fun teasing each other and laughing at each other's antics. As I watched, I became so caught up in their enjoyment that I ran up to the boys and asked them if I could join them, as I also wanted very much to dive off these towering walls of rocks like they were doing. They told me I was too young and too small to be diving into the deep water. Later, when they were getting ready to leave, they told me to leave the area, as I might fall in the water and drown. They laughed at my foolishness to even suggest I could dive like they did. I left feeling very discouraged and upset at being rejected. As I walked home, I started planning to return the following morning and try diving when the boys were not around, just to prove them wrong.

The next morning, I went alone to practice diving off those rocks. The weather was perfect; a gentle breeze blew over the water, and the sun was very hot. It was a good day to swim, and the big boys were not around to tell me where I could or couldn't swim. The only sounds I was aware of were the water lapping gently on the rocks, the leaves gently flapping in the breeze, and a dog barking in the distance. I took my first dive from about two feet above the water level, and it wasn't that hard after all. I was really starting to enjoy the cool water on my body and the rush I experienced when I hit the water from the higher positions. I made several successful dives. Then I got brave and decided to go all the way to the highest rock, which was about 6 meters (20 feet) high and try diving from there. I remember standing on that high rock overlooking the water, and it seemed very high from this vantage point. I must have stood there for a long time becoming very afraid of how far away the water surface seemed.

I had nearly aborted my attempted dive when I remembered the laughter of the big boys when I'd suggested that I could dive from the rocks like them. I decided I was going to do this and surprise those big boys the next time they came swimming here. At this moment, I sprang into the air. I was going down quite quickly, but time seemed to stand still as I watched the water slowly approaching. I hit the water perfectly and didn't realize how fast I was now traveling through the water.

Suddenly, I saw the bottom of the lake coming up to meet my face too rapidly for me to avoid contact and I hit the bottom of the lake with my forehead, snapping my head backwards. I felt a sharp pain in my lower back and, at the same time, I heard the crack of my spine on impact. I lost the ability to coordinate my movements in the water and I could see the bright sunlight above on the water surface. In spite of the pain I was experiencing, I attempted to swim towards the surface, but I felt like I was not moving forward. It seemed as if I was in the water a long time, and I was starting to feel I needed air—*right now*! I couldn't hold my breath any longer, so I inhaled and immediately felt the cold water rush into my throat and lungs; my lungs felt cool as I inhaled the water deeply. I was losing sight of the water surface, and I could feel the inside of my chest getting cold. All I could see was red; everything was turning red, and it seemed like I was dreaming or already in a dream.

I awoke that afternoon lying on a sandy beach, and I could feel the hot sun on my back. Half of my face and body were still lying in the water. I started coughing and vomiting water; I don't know how long I lay there. I didn't feel any pain; now I felt normal. When I was able to stand up, I realized I was on the west side of the point by my father's fuel storage house on the hill. I had somehow ended up around the point from the north side to the west side. I walked across the point to where I had left my clothes, got dressed, and went home. I arrived home and found out what time of day it was when my mother informed me that I had missed dinner and she wanted to know if I had eaten at someone else's home.

"I wasn't hungry," I replied. The realization suddenly hit me that it was already late afternoon! I didn't tell Mom where I had been, and I never mentioned this experience to my mom or dad. To this day, I still don't know how I survived the incident, especially having been submerged in the water that long and ending up so far from where I had been diving.

Each time I thought about this, my first and only thoughts immediately went to Mother; Grandma; and my Sunday school teacher, Mr. Smith, who was a good friend of my father. All three often told me that they were praying for me. When Mom and I visited Grandma during the summer months, Grandma would often start her evening prayers with a petition on my behalf for my safety and protection, especially when I was sitting beside her. I used to think that she was just doing that to please me. I am now convinced that those prayers were answered—that they continued ringing in God's ears, that He reacted to that request, and that by His grace I remain alive today. My only regret is that I didn't tell my mother and grandma that their prayers were answered before they passed on.

Later on in my life, I would be submitted to pre-employment X-rays. Every time, the doctors who viewed my X-rays would ask what year it was that I had broken my back, and my answer would always be the same— that I didn't ever recall having broken any bones in my back. They would explain that the heavy build-up of calcium on my spine told otherwise. I am sure they checked my provincial medical records and did not find any evidence of spinal injuries.

Going to school in Oxford House, where I started at the age of seven, involved a daily walk of about two miles each way. During my first two years, I walked with my brother, John since he attended the same school. The school was one big classroom into which all the students from grades one through eight crowded. The classes were divided by rows, with the lowest grades sitting up front near the teacher's desk. One teacher taught all the school grades, and I can imagine he or she was a very busy person. All the kids started their schooling with the same handicap—not being able to understand or speak the English language.

The first English word that I learned was *cat*, which I was able to learn from my dad's older storekeeper, Bill, who tried to teach me the language. I probably would have picked up a few more English words had he started to teach me a little sooner, not to mention if I had been a bit more interested in learning this new language. I did not realize that someday I would need to speak this language. Most of what I'd been taught in grades one and two was in the Cree language, so English had not been a problem for me just yet.

The teacher had a helper who spent time with the beginners, and she always spoke to us in Cree. Most of my activities in those first two years involved learning to play games and drawing illustrations of what we did at home or at play, but I don't recall learning any English.

John, who was eight years older, would tell me what the teacher had said or wanted. The older kids were taught in English, but they didn't speak it unless they had to.

The only part of the school I liked at that time was the noon hour since it was the only time we could stay at our desks when the teacher was not around. John brought and kept both our lunches, and he would give me my sandwich when it was time to eat. One of the senior students was put in charge, and boy did he report everything that went on during the lunch hour when the teacher was absent from the room. Of course the teacher was in the other part of the building set aside for the teacher's accommodations having his lunch.

There were times during the lunch hour that I became a wise guy, and sometimes the teacher would talk to me about it on my behind and that wasn't too bad; it hurt my pride more than my bottom. The school also had a disciplinarian who would be called to the school to deal with a disobedient child. The parents of the child sometimes showed up with the disciplinarian, and that meant double trouble for the kid involved. Having other family members in the same classroom did not give one any slack since the parents would hear about the day's activities from one of their other kids.

One time, I got a severe strapping from the teacher for disobeying. We were told never to leave the playgrounds when we were attending school, but another boy and I decided to go down to the lake shore to see if the lake had frozen over yet. We knew that we were leaving the school grounds, but we were only going to have a quick peek and be right back. No sooner had we arrived and started playing on the newly formed ice than we forgot the time. Disobedience and disrespect was not tolerated in this school system.

When I arrived home, I was careful not to open the palms of my hands to reveal the blisters from my strapping. I knew that I would get punished again if my parents found out that I had been disobedient. My father had warned me on my first day of school that he would punish me if I ever got disciplined for disobedience. I felt very pleased with myself for having successfully concealed the evidence of my discipline. I made it through supper and the evening family gathering in the living room without my parents finding out. Our family gathering consisted of going over each person's activities and concerns for that day, and if a need arose, my father or mother would plan to take action to meet that need. Otherwise, it was an opportunity for my parents to tell us of any news they had received from other family members.

I had lain down on the floor by the warm stove, feeling very good about myself as no one had suspected anything. I had fallen asleep when my oldest sister Rosie walked by and saw the blisters on my hands. She immediately called out to my mother, asking her how I'd blistered my hands. I awoke with a start when I realized what Rosie was saying. Both my parents were beside me immediately, and they knew right away how I'd gotten the blisters. I had to fess up right then and there. My dad told me that he would deal with this tomorrow, and that didn't mean going to the school to talk to the teacher about being cruel to me. I don't know if I slept the rest of that night since I was worried about what my dad would do to me.

I came home the next day from school, and I tried to convince my mother that she should be the one dealing with this instead of my father, as he was too busy to be bothered with me. I knew she would not punish me physically like my dad would. It was obvious to me that she was as grieved as I was over this matter. I am sure she was feeling sorry for me; however, my pleas did not work. I suspected she'd already tried talking Dad out of my punishment. I finally left to see Dad in his shop. When I arrived at the shop, my dad was talking with a couple of customers. He told me our talk would have to wait until the following day, as he was very busy right then. That was not what I wanted to hear since now I would spend another sleepless night worrying about what he would do to me.

The next day, I went back down to my father's shop and found him working alone making cabinets for newlyweds in the community. He made me sit and wait until he was done with what he was working on, and that must have taken about an hour. During that hour, I sat in complete agitation, squirming, worrying, and sweating bullets, wondering what punishment I would be receiving. That hour seemed like an eternity for me, and I just wanted it to end, as I felt my stomach developing those huge knots. My tension was finally relieved when Dad told me that he felt the punishment the teacher had given me was sufficient. He then gave me a long lecture about the importance of being obedient, and I made sure to let him know that I would try not to disobey the teacher again. It was times like this, when he was being lenient, that I felt he must have loved me more than I could ever understand, and that always made me feel repentant and ashamed for disobeying.

However, it seemed I had a problem of forgetting what had happened the last time I disobeyed. Therefore, I was always on my best behaviour when in school, as I didn't want my dad topping off any punishments I might get at school. My father and I agreed after our last meeting that I was supposed to tell him if I got disciplined at school again. I eventually realized that obedience was what built a person's nature, character, and reputation, which I admired in my father. I often look back with regret at the many times I ignorantly and blindly entered the area of disobedience, without considering the effects my actions may have on others.

I was eight years old when my two nephews and I were punished for lying to Bill, the store clerk. We had gone to my father's store to ask Bill for cigarettes that I said my father wanted.

"What brand did your dad ask for?" Bill asked me.

"The yellow package they call Mill Banks," I replied, as my nephews and I had rehearsed what I was going to say.

"Did he want matches as well?" asked Bill.

"Yes, he needs those as well," I lied.

We left the store and headed down to the lake shore to a boat that was in storage for the winter, as it was covered over with a tarp. My nephews and I opened the package, and we started to light each other's cigarettes. I sat with my back against the side of the boat and was in the process of taking my first puff when I looked up and there was my father standing there looking at us. I immediately felt my heart stop, the blood drained from my face, and I couldn't breathe. I was so overcome with fear that I couldn't even call out to my nephews to warn them that we had been caught red-handed.

"Bill came down to the mill to ask if I received the cigarettes I had sent for," he said. "I was very surprised when he told me that you said I needed cigarettes, so I came looking for you. But I can see those cigarettes were not for me," he said with anger rising in his voice. "I want you all to come out of there, and we will all go to the house and tell your mothers what you were doing," he said. He waved for us to come out. "Bill watched you walking in the opposite direction from where he knew I was, so he came to tell me what you had said and where you boys had gone," he continued. Disappointment showed on Dad's face, and his voice started to reveal anger and frustration.

My mother was just horrified that we would lie to Bill and steal cigarettes; she was hurt by this revelation. My father asked her to go and get Rosie so she could deal with her boys. We all got spanked, and I was sent to bed immediately without lunch and supper. My mother checked on me once in a while, but she never said a word to me in all that time.

The following day at noon, my father came home and said to me, "Get up now and wash yourself. We will lunch together so we can talk."

I got up, dreading the meeting at the dining room table. My mother sat quietly in the kitchen when I came in and sat down at my usual place across from my father at the dining room table. Mom brought me my lunch, and I could see that she had been crying. I was just crushed at seeing her pain, and I didn't feel hungry anymore.

"Have you considered what you have done?" Dad asked, looking at me with pity and disappointment. Then he continued, "What you have done was serious. People go to prisons for stealing and lying like you did. I hope this has been a lesson that you will remember for the rest of your life. Now eat your lunch, and I will hear your answer after you have eaten."

I ate my food as instructed, eating in silence and ashamed of what I had done. Above all, I was hurting inside, realizing I had disappointed and hurt my mother. I could not get rid of the memory of that horrified look on her face when she'd heard what I had done yesterday. That picture would forever be in my memory. Finally, I finished my food even though I wasn't hungry, as my stomach was still tied up in knots. I said, starting to cry, "I really feel bad for what I did, and I still don't know why I did it." I stopped talking then, and I started shaking, as I was overwhelmed with sorrow and guilt. I know my father could sense the regret I felt over what I had done, and I am sure he saw the grief that was written all over my face. I am also sure he could see my hurt each time Mom came near me while she served us lunch. My tears were always threatening to flow each time I looked and saw the disappointment and hurt on her face.

"I want you to go and see Bill and apologize for lying to him. I am sure he will forgive you, like your mother and I will," Dad instructed.

"I will go and see him today," I said, as Mom came in and sat beside me.

My father got up to leave. "I will tell Bill you will drop by to see him later," he said. "Remember, your mother and I love you, and we will always do what's best for you," he added as he put his hand on my shoulder and gave me a light squeeze with a smile.

While he was walking towards the door, my mother put her arms around me, kissed my cheek, then gave me a squeeze and asked, "Can I get you dessert?"

"I can't eat anymore right now, but I will have some later after I talk to Bill," I replied.

I was worried and trying to build up the courage to go and see Bill. I was wondering what his reaction would be when I confessed and asked for his forgiveness. I was afraid he would be angry with me and refuse to talk to me.

About a half hour went by before I decided to just walk over there and make my apology, no matter the outcome. When I arrived at the store, I did not see Bill around so I called out to him. Bill answered me from the basement where he was putting a few more logs into the furnace. I went down and made my apology to him, and I asked him to forgive me.

"Of course I forgive you. Anyone who can get up enough courage to admit he did wrong deserves to be forgiven," Bill said. "I was never angry with you, Morris, as I have made many mistakes too. And you know what? The hardest part for me was to admit my faults to the ones I have hurt most," he said with a smile and a wink of reassurance.

I came away relieved, with a promise to myself that I would always be on guard and think before I acted. I saw my nephews the following day, and they told me that they had gotten another spanking from their dad when they got home.

One beautiful, warm spring day, my nephews and I got into trouble again. I was eight years old, Lawrence was seven, and Bobby was six. The kids in our community were told by our parents that we were never to walk on the lake ice during spring break-up since we could fall through the ice and drown. At the end of another school day, Lawrence, Bobby, and I were walking along the shoreline with the other kids from the same school. We were on our way home from school when we decided it would be fun to jump on the pieces of ice that were floating by. Once we started moving from one piece of ice to the next, we decided we could cross the lake this way and we would get home a lot quicker. Some of the broken pieces of ice we jumped onto were only 1 meter (39 inches) in diameter; these would begin to sink when under our weight, so we would quickly jump onto the next piece. My feet were getting wet from not jumping off the smaller pieces quickly enough, and the water went over and into my ankle boots.

We'd gotten about a quarter of the way across the lake when my mother saw us on the ice flow. She started screaming at us to turn back. As she was shrieking in a very high-pitched voice, it was obvious that she was very angry and worried. We each jumped onto larger pieces of floating ice so we could stop, stand still, listen, and observe our surroundings. We quickly decided to turn back as ordered, and we eventually made it back to the shore safely.

We then walked home around the shoreline road silently, solemnly, and with a sombre expression clearly on each of our faces, knowing what now awaited us at home. We tried reassuring one another that we may just get a lecture about the dangers of moving ice, but I don't think anyone of us believed that for a moment.

Once I arrived home, my mother was waiting for me. She started scolding me in a loud, high-pitched, and shaky voice, saying, "You and Rosie's boys could have fallen off the floating ice chunks and gotten crushed or drowned in that cold water! You were told time after time that you are never to go on the ice after the ice crossings were shut down for the spring break-up," she cried, her voice quivering with rage. She continued with tears running down her cheeks, still yelling, "I was so afraid that you boys were all going to drown when I saw you standing on those broken pieces of ice out in the middle of the lake! I thought I wouldn't see you again until your body was recovered from the water, and we had to prepare you for burial." She wiped the tears from her eyes, and her voice returned to normal. She was still shaking and upset from witnessing our ordeal, and I kept silent while she scolded me.

I was feeling terrible for what we'd done and that my disobedience was once again hurting my mother and probably my father too. I was okay with her scolding me since I deserved it. But when she mentioned that she had told Dad, I became very afraid. "You better go and see your father now; he told me to send you to his shop as soon as you got home," she said.

I spent the next fifteen minutes performing my best begging techniques (crying, begging, promising to be perfect, and the like) to persuade her not to send me to see Dad, but that didn't work. I started walking slowly towards the shop.

When I walked in, I saw Rosie there with Lawrence and Bobby, and I knew we were done for. Poor Rosie looked like she was ready to cry, and she was looking for my father's support in dealing with this matter since Sam was not at home right then. She looked at me with pitiful eyes, and that's when I saw her concern and outrage at what we had done. Her expression also showed the love she had for us, and it was beginning to be obvious the disappointment she felt was starting to overwhelm her. She loved her boys very much and only wanted the very best for them, and she knew our father would give her the advice and guidance she needed at this time. I realized at that moment that she was still my father's little girl, who stood there looking to her father for guidance, support, and a decision; she wanted to discipline her boys in a way that ensured they would learn the consequences of their disobedience.

My nephews and I received a very serious lecture and a spanking from my father which we deserved. I was sent home immediately after that and told to go straight to bed without supper. I found out the next day from my two nephews that they'd gotten another spanking from their dad when he'd returned home that evening.

I look back now and think that it must have broken my dad's heart each time he disciplined me, as he always displayed a lot of love for me, even after I became an adult. I think those were the times my attitude took shape and the patterns of my behaviour were established.

Thinking back later, I would realize that my attitude improved after that incident. I compared myself to my brother, John, whom I thought had perfected the art of obedience; he continually received favour from my parents as a result of his obedience. I, on the other hand, was always messing up, getting caught, and being found guilty of disobedience; as a result, I was always getting punished for it. I realized that my parents would find it very challenging to be proud of a son who was always being disobedient, so I decided to watch and listen to John and hoped some of his attitude would rub off on me. Dad and Mom were always expressing their confidence in John, and I wanted them to be like that with me. I remember thinking after that last incident that I needed to change my attitude to make my parents proud.

I have acquired many scars on my body as a result of my foolishness. For example, when we were swinging on a large swing that one of my brothers had made for us in a field near our house, my nephews and I decided to see who could jump the farthest off the swing. Earlier, I had noticed a board lying in the tall grass, which we all continued to ignore. My final jump I thought would make history by being the longest jump in the history of humankind. I landed on the board, which had a rusty four-inch nail protruding upward from it. I landed on this nail, which went straight through my foot. The pain was so great I nearly passed out. As usual, my mother heard my scream and came to my aid. She removed the rusty nail, cleaned and bandaged the wound, and comforted me, assuring me that I would heal again.

I experienced another moment of pain during the winter months when my nephews and I were walking by the sawmill. I went to see the large, shiny, circular saw on the mill, and to this day, I don't know why I stuck out my tongue and touched the saw blade. I am assuming that, because it looked so clean and shiny, I must have wondered what it would taste like, so I took a sample. My tongue immediately stuck onto the blade, and I was trapped like a squirrel, until my tongue warmed the metal and some of the flesh partially loosened. My nephews didn't know what to do; nor could they help me to remove my tongue from that blade. Normally, we could come up with all kinds of good solutions when we had a problem since we all had great imaginations. However, our solutions in this case were more silly than good. We briefly considered them running home, a distance of a kilometre, to get water, which they would need to boil before returning and pouring it on the blade and my tongue. Pouring the hot boiling water on the blade and my tongue, my nephews figured, would permit the two stuck parts that were held together by frost to release, *simple*!

I couldn't listen any longer to all the chatter and excitement and more suggestions, so I pulled my tongue off the saw blade, leaving my donation of flesh stuck to the blade. My tongue immediately started bleeding, and it felt like a hot iron was being placed on my tongue. I tried using snow to absorb the blood and cool my tongue. The cold snow applied to my tongue brought a little relief.

I was not able to eat normal foods for several days, and my diet consisted of soft, lukewarm foods. My mother felt sorry for me, and she said it was a lesson that I would not soon forget. My father was away on a business trip at the time. When spring came, my father would probably wonder how all that flesh had gotten on his clean, shiny saw blade, and I had probably discovered a new diet that I could have advertised in one of those fashion magazines. My tongue healed quickly, and my mother was right— it was a lesson I would never forget.

Chapter 8
Grandma Nellie Poker

MY GRANDMOTHER, NELLIE POKER, was a strong Christian woman who never got discouraged when trouble crossed her path. And yet she was a very humble person, always thinking of other people's needs before her own. She had one sister and one brother, Bella York and James Hall. During the evening prayers, it seemed she prayed for everyone on this earth, and I would often get impatient and start playing. I would somehow get my Cousin Eleanor's attention so I could make funny faces to make her laugh. She always thought I was funny, until I would receive an angry glare from my mother and then I would be quiet again.

Different members of Grandma's family came over to her house each night to take part in her evening prayers. Grandma Nellie would start praying on bended knees; then she would sit for a while before getting back on her knees. All the while I'd noted the sun's rays moving across the floor and the big hand on her clock making a complete circle past the point where it had started. She would spend a lot of her prayer hours thanking her God and expressing her admiration for His love and mercy towards her, her family, and community. She truly feared, loved, and admired this judge of all the earth, who had created humankind from the dust of the earth.

This Almighty God she communicated with always brought a sense of fear to my heart, as I was overwhelmed to hear how mighty and all-powerful He was. And yet, I felt a desire to hear more of Him, as she described Him in her prayers. I believe Grandma Poker had an impact on my life, since I was with her during those early years of my childhood. I would often think of her and wish I could have the same joy she had in her daily life. She had a laughter that made me smile when I heard it, as only Grandma could laugh like that.

When I was at my grandmother's home during our summer visits, I would sit quietly watching her during her personal devotion when no was else was around. I was captivated by her sincere worship, and I admired the faith, courage, and joy this woman had. She lived alone in a big house she'd once shared with her husband and children. After my grandfather left for the sanatorium, all Grandma had left were her children and friends. She did not speak English, and the cost of travel in those days was prohibitive; she was living on a fixed budget. I never got to see my grandfather, as he had passed away while I was still an infant. Her children and friends were all she had left, and all her children were now married and lived in their own homes raising their families. Some of her children lived in the same community, while others, like Mom, lived elsewhere. Those who lived in the same community made their daily visits just to check on her, while those living elsewhere would visit as often as they could. My father, mother, and I would visit her during the summer months while my brothers and sisters who were at home would stay at home at Oxford House helping around the store and yard.

Grandma Nellie was a very independent person and wouldn't think of living in anybody else's home. She did her own daily chores, such as chopping wood for her kitchen wood stove. She exercised daily by taking long, fast walks just to keep in shape; as a child, I couldn't go along as I was not able to keep up with her.

When I was very young, I recognized the love my mother had for her mother in the things she said and did for Grandma. A smile would immediately appear on my mother's face when I told her of the things Grandma could do and how proud I was of her.

My grandma worked hard doing her own work, along with making clothing for other people. I credit a lot of my life's success to hard work as a result of the influence I received from my parents and Grandma. Seeing a person living alone was new to me, and I was amazed that she could survive. She was a very happy person, always humming or telling me funny stories just to make me laugh. When a neighbour, friend, or one of her daughters came over, she would immediately stop whatever she was doing and focus all her attention on that visitor. Just watching her and listening to her encouraging others made me realize that there was nothing I couldn't do. I enjoyed being around Grandma, and as I grew older during those summers with her, I would always walk away with a new spring in my step, knowing that, with my Creator's help, I could do all things through him who strengthens me. The faith and joy that Grandma had is now mine as well.

Grandma Nellie lived by a small creek in Rossville on the Norway House Cree Nation. Thinking back later, I would wonder how she was able to cope without her husband around since she talked much about him, and I sensed that she missed him very much. I wondered if she was aware that she would never see him again in this life. I truly believe that it was her faith in God that kept her encouraged. She did all the work and chores around the house when we were not with her. Of course, her other daughters and their children who lived close by did what they could to help her.

I will always keep her memory in my heart, as she always made special time for me and would take me with her when she went grocery shopping or visiting friends. She included me in everything she did. She would make sure her friends or distant relatives got to meet me. I remember the special moments we shared when she was baking, and she would name all the ingredients as if I would remember them. I was always the first person to sample her baking when it was done, and that made me feel very special.

Chapter 9
The Sawmill

MY FATHER SOLD LUMBER, which was manufactured at his lumber mill locally at Oxford House. One winter when I was about eight years old, I had the opportunity to help my brother John who was hauling some lumber to the Catholic mission. The mission had purchased the lumber for a new church building the church membership was planning to build in the spring. I enjoyed riding on the snowmobile that pulled the sled holding the lumber. We made several trips, and each trip was as much fun as the first. I didn't even mind helping John unload and pile the boards neatly at the delivery point.

During the summer months, I was allowed to help around the sawmill when it was operating; I was given a job helping cut the slabs or feeding two-by-four boards into the planer. I dreaded being there on nice days, as all the other kids would spend the days swimming. One of the ways I used to get out of work was to take advantage of my mother's fear of me getting hurt. When she came to see how I was doing, I pretended not to see her and would stick my fingers close to the spinning blades on the planer, and she would get worried and express her concerns to Dad, who would then tell me I could go and play with my friends.

My father and his employees hauled the logs across the lake to the sawmill by constructing them into large rafts that could be pushed by boats powered by outboard motors. On arrival, the men would then release the logs and tie them together and secure them to the shore to prevent them from floating away. Dad had hired construction contractors to drill and install anchor bolts into the bedrock so the logs could be pulled up on a slide onto the mill cutting table. The horses were used for pulling the logs out of the water, and these logs were neatly piled in front of the mill slide.

I was curious as to why these men came, so I spent one morning watching the miners drill holes in the rocks. Two men held the drill rod while the third man struck the top of the rod, and with each strike, the men holding the drill rod would turn the rod a few degrees. I was just amazed that these miners could hit the rod every time and not the man holding the rod. The men used water pressured by a little pump to flush out the holes. They then lowered the anchor bolts into the holes and secured them by tightening an expansion bolt that was threaded onto the bottom of the bolt. These bolts could be reused, but I never saw them removed once they were installed. These bolts were located in various locations so the logs could be pulled up sideways onto the slide and onto the cutting table and the mill carriage. The carriage moved each log into the saw to cut it into lumber. Once the full length of the log was cut, the carriage moved back to the starting point, the log was turned by the metal teeth holding the log, and the next length of board was cut, and so on. I used to sit off to the side and watch from a distance as the powerful saw buzzed through those logs, thinking that someday, when I grew up, I would work in a sawmill.

My father was planning to build cement platforms at the sawmill the following summer, so my brother John was given the job of hauling gravel from the gravel pit across the lake. He used the dog team to haul the gravel on a sleigh during early spring when the ice was starting to melt. The route he was to follow was along the shoreline road. After a few trips, he decided to travel directly across the lake on the ice. Travelling directly across was a shorter route, and it was easier traveling on the bare ice. The dogs were able to travel much faster on the ice than they could on the snow-covered road, and they didn't have to work as hard.

John was returning home on his final trip several days later when the sled went through the ice, pulling the dog team down with it. This team was harnessed in a straight formation so the dogs were in a straight line, which made travelling on trails through the bush roads in snow easy. The rear dog was closest to the sled, about two feet from the front of it, so that dog was the first in the water when the sled went down. Four of the dogs behind him were pulled in too. John jumped into the water to cut the dogs loose so they would not drown. He was able to save the dog team, and fortunately, another dog team was behind him to rush him home before he got too cold. The dogs that had fallen in ran home to their warm kennels and were waiting for their food when John found them. The cold water didn't seem to bother them, as they just shook it off their coats.

The next morning, I went along with John and George and my father to pull the sled out of the water. The location where the sled had gone down had frozen over during the night, so they had to chop a hole to get the sled out. The early morning hours were the best time for this type of work since the ice had not started melting yet. I was very proud of my brother John as he could have easily stood back and watched the team drown while he stayed dry. But he didn't; he felt he had to do what was right, even after realizing that the panicking dogs could have easily pulled him under water, endangering his own safety. He also knew how valuable the dogs were to our dad's work. As his little brother, I knew he would be there for me too if I ever needed his help.

I enjoyed watching the horses my father used to pull the logs out of the water up the hill to the sawmill. Some of the logs were so big and heavy that I would stop to watch to see if the horses could pull these logs, and I was always amazed at their strength. My dad often released the sawmill horses to wander and graze over the weekends. Other horses, whose owners had released them, came around our place, and they would all graze and stay together.

One Sunday afternoon, my two older brothers spent several hours trying to catch the horses to go riding. The horses from the mill must have known it was Sunday, which was their day off. Just when my brothers decided to give up the chase, my father came out of the house and walked towards the dock to check on his boat. The horses liked him since he would often have treats, and the horses went and walked with my dad, expecting a treat from him. This is when my brothers were able to catch the horses for their afternoon ride.

There were times one couldn't get near my dad's shop, as these horses would crowd around the door entrance, waiting for a treat. Like me, some of the locals were very afraid of these horses since they were new to our community and the majority of the people had never seen a horse. I think they thought the horses were like wild animals and would be unpredictable. If the horses were grazing by the store on the green grass, the locals would turn back and go home rather than walk by them. There was always another day for shopping.

Chapter 10
My Father's Friends and Customers

A S A CHILD LIVING in Oxford House, I saw some very interesting people who came to do business with my dad. Dad considered these customers his friends. One person I always admired for his courage and determination was a man who was crippled from birth; he was not able to straighten his legs and stand on his feet. I knew him by his Cree nickname, Cheepos. I believe his last name was Nattaway. Many of the people in Oxford House had Cree nicknames, and as their Christian and surnames were never used, I never knew their real names.

Being physically handicapped didn't stop Cheepos from being a trapper and dog musher; he lived and travelled alone in the north. His laughter indicated that he was a very happy person, and the reality of his physical condition did not seem to affect his joy or his work. Because of his inability to straighten out his legs, he would move along on all fours on his hands and bent legs. I was surprised how well he was able to move along at a good pace. This man had trained his dog team to pull his sleigh so he could get around on his trapline during the winter months.

During the summer months, when he lived in the community, Cheepos had his dogs pull a wagon he'd purchased so he could get around the community. The dog team understood his every command, and the lead dog was very obedient. When Cheepos stopped to talk to someone, the dogs would sit or lay down, and they didn't seem to get impatient like most dogs did; in addition, these dogs were not aggressive and mean like most of the huskies I saw. This trapper was a very friendly person, whose joyful laugher could be heard from a distance as he talked with a neighbour. He treated his dogs with respect. He would often sit and talk to them as if they understood his every word; he treated them like they were his best friends, and one could see that he loved them very much. No doubt they protected him from the hungry wolves and bears on his trapline. He lived alone in his trapper's cabin and made a good living from trapping; he was always well dressed. I never talked to him much, as I often just observed while my brothers or my father did all the talking and never interrupted or engaged in adult conversations.

Another of the gentleman who frequented Dad's store was different in quite another way. He grew hair all over his body, including his face. I was afraid of him because I thought he looked more like an animal than a man. His hair covered his face completely, not like a man with a beard. The hair was on his nose and around his eyes, forehead, and ears; he also had hair on his hands. Most, if not all, people in our community were afraid of him. As kids, we were afraid to go near him, let alone talk to him. I would never see another human being like that.

Now that I am older, I can still see him in my mind and think that he must have been a very lonely person. I never saw him at any of the community activities, and I remember this one day I was outside by myself when he walked up to me on his way to see my dad. I did not see nor hear him approaching. I turned to see who was there when his shadow darkened the sun where I was sitting. When I looked up and saw who it was, I froze instantly with fear. I was not able to speak or move or yell for help because I was so terrified. He probably saw how frightened I was, so he just walked on by. I ran into the house once he was out of sight and stayed there until I knew he was gone. After that experience, he often appeared in my dreams, and even then just seeing him again frightened me.

I used to watch from a safe distance as this man talked to my dad, and the two visited and enjoyed each other's company. I can understand why this man came to see my father often since they seemed to be good friends.

He had large dogs on his dog team that were made up mostly of cross-breeds (half wolf, half dog). He would warn people not to come close to his dogs since they were unpredictable. I'm sure this is because they weren't used to people, as they never saw another human being once they left the community. I am assuming that the dogs had a fear of people like they had of wild animals. One day, my schoolmates and I were going home from school; we were walking along a trail by the lake when we met this man and his dog team. When he saw us, he told us to wait as he moved his dogs off the trail to let us by; he didn't want anyone to come close to the dogs. The dogs were snarling and showing us their teeth as we walked by, which made me very afraid.

The man with the hair wasn't the only one of my dad's customers who I feared because of his physical abnormalities. I remember one large and strong man who did not have a voice box and so was not able to talk. His Cree name was Stomian, and his Christian name was Jimmy Weenusk. He would grunt and motion with his hands to communicate. I used to watch him communicating with my dad and somehow they understood one another. My dad often repaired Stomian's outboard motor for him. I never got to know this man as I kept my distance because I was afraid of him. This was probably because of the loud grunting noises he made when he tried to communicate. This man lived in the village and often came to visit my dad in his shop to spend the afternoon with him. I learned from watching these people that whatever obstacles come our way, they could be overcome.

My parents had many other friends with whom they spent time, and these friends came from all walks of life. I know my parents appreciated every one of their friends. Often, our house had visitors in the evenings, and everyone was always welcome. There was never a time when it was too late or my parents had other plans; they catered to others and enjoyed friendship. Some of these people travelled long distances for visits.

I remember one woman, a Mrs. Mitchell, the wife of a game warden, who used to come from across the lake to visit my mother. Mrs. Mitchell drove her dog team all by herself. She wore long moose-hide mitts with lots of fancy beadwork that could tell a story. I used to admire the art designs on her mitts and came to the conclusion that she must have spent several days making those mitts. I was often playing outside when she came out of our house with her fancy parka and moose-hide mitts to tackle the – 30°F (– 34.44°C) weather outside. She harnessed and handled those dogs as well as a man; I was truly impressed.

The people of Oxford House I knew were very honest and hard-working people. Their determination and desire to accomplish their goals was always evident in their commitment and efforts. I watched the men pack heavy loads along portages, and I listened to their discussions at the sawmill, as they planned ways to get their jobs done better and smarter. They were team players at work and in life, just like they were on the soccer field, determined to win the game. As a child, I was often impressed by their outward display of concern for one another; they continuously encouraged one another as if they were family. They had good senses of humour, often saying something to make each other laugh. When one was struggling under a heavy load of timber, others would drop what they were doing and quickly come to his aid. One could hear their laughter from a distance, and I often enjoyed listening to them work.

Recently, while visiting the community of Norway House, which was celebrating its annual York Boat Days, I received word that the Oxford House team was going to take part in the York boat races, so I went to watch the races. Some of the onlookers commented that the Oxford House team did not stand a chance as these types of races were always won by local teams, who were proficient in handling the big boats. Oxford House, I was told, only knew how to paddle canoes. The Oxford House team did not win the race that day, and I believe I may have been the only person cheering for them. I told some of the onlookers that this Oxford House team would come back and win in a year or two since now they knew what they had to do to win. Some of the guys doubted this, as Norway House had a long history of using these boats. I was depending on my memory of the Oxford House people, whom I knew would not back down and give up just because they lost this one race. I remembered they were team players full of encouragement for one another, and I knew they would return with a game plan.

That same team from Oxford House came back to Norway House a year later and won the race. I received word of their accomplishment via a telephone call from a spectator in Norway House. I knew then that the people of Oxford House still had the tenacity and determination their fathers and grandfathers had. I was very proud of them.

Chapter 11
Our Neighbours at Oxford House

AT ABOUT A KILOMETRE away, the Catholic mission was the closest building to our home. Fr. Daniel and the mission worker, a brother, next door were very good neighbours; they were always looking out for those who lived nearby. One winter night, they were pounding on our back door trying to wake up my folks as they had noticed a fire blazing out of our furnace chimney on the roof. It turned out that the soot build-up inside the chimney had caught on fire, and the furnace pipes were glowing red hot and had started a fire in the attic.

My dad, my brothers, the brother, and Father Daniel all helped cut a hole in the ceiling to gain access to the fire, so they could put it out. There was no fire department in our community back then. My dad got inside the ceiling, and the other men handed him buckets of water to throw at the fire. It must have been smoky inside the attic; he was not hitting the burning area with the pails of water he was throwing, as, I assumed, he could not see. The priest then got up into the attic through another hole on the low part of the attic ceiling to give Dad directions. Fr. Daniels put himself in the line of fire. Following the direction of Fr. Daniel's voice, my dad directed the water towards him. After he'd thrown a few pails in the direction of the priest, the fire was finally put out.

The ceiling was dripping with water, as was the priest's beard, which had had a couple of pails of water thrown at it. Fr. Daniels made it look like he was wringing out his beard like you would a rag. I am sure that little performance was especially for me, as that made me smile.

Fortunately, we had more than one stove in our big house, so the house could be kept warm after the ceiling hole was covered. Mom made tea and put out some pastry for everyone to enjoy while drying off. The unfortunate situation was turned into a good time, which made everyone feel appreciated. We did not have running water then, so the water Dad used was from the cooking and washing water reservoirs. Now that these reservoirs were low, my brothers would be hauling water again the next morning. The furnace pipes were replaced, and the ceiling was repaired during the next couple days.

Fr. Daniel and the brother who assisted him were good friends and neighbours of my parents. As a little boy, I would often be found playing at the mission, as most of my other friends at that time were Catholics. The brother at the mission would always entertain us during those beautiful warm summer days by reading the newspaper comics to us, which were written in French; he would translate them into Cree for us. My favourite was the little boy in the comics named Henry. I can still hear the soft, rhythmic sound of the gentle breeze setting the leaves overhead aflutter. The benches were located directly under one of the large birch trees beside the log chapel where the brother used to read the comics to us. I never did find out the brother's name, as we always referred to him as "brother" in Cree (Nistes, with an accent on the "e"). This Catholic brother would often organize soccer games for us, or we would just help him do his daily chores.

During the hot afternoons, we would all go for a swim, often playing ballgames in the shallow waters near the mission, which was blessed with a beautiful, sandy beach. Some days, we spent our time playing soccer in the field by the mission since the older boys didn't mind us kids playing on their teams, as long as we could put up with their rough plays. I can still feel the sting of the ball on my body when I blocked a kick from a cornered player. These games would go on late into the evening, and we would quit when it got too dark to see the ball. We didn't mind the clouds of mosquitoes feeding on us as we played; now I am bothered by one mosquito flying by my ear.

My summer recreation also included boating since my father had provided me with my own flat-bottomed rowboat to use on the lake by our home. My nephews and I would spend days floating around the shorelines chasing fish in the shallow waters or just exploring along the lake shore. We sometimes transported someone across the bay to the nursing station if they asked us, and we never turned anyone down. We would also go along with one of our friends and his father on a wild chicken hunt in a forest nearby. When a bird was shot, we would all race to be the first to pick up the bird and carry it to my friend's home. In that way, we felt we had played a part in the successful hunt.

My life was filled with excitement during my childhood, and every kid I knew was my friend. The summers were filled with exciting adventures. We made some of our own toys and slingshots. We would race down to the stone pebble shore and load our pockets with stones to be used for ammunition during our hunts. We hunted the birds, and during all those years, I remember getting one robin. I felt so badly that we had a special burial service for it, and I apologized to the dead bird for killing it. I believe that ended my career as a bird hunter.

My bedroom window faced the east side of the lake, and I would often look out the window on a sunny morning during the summer to watch the sun glistening on the water. During the winter mornings after waking up, I would sit on my bed admiring the sunbeams reflecting off the tops of the snowdrifts on the lake. During the daytime, the sun would be strong enough to melt the south side of the snowdrifts that reflected the sun, adding to the beauty of the winter scene. My parents were early risers. When 7:00 a.m. came along, I was just getting out of bed, and my father would have already left to work in the mill or in his shop.

The older boys from our village used to hunt wild spruce hens or the Sharp-tailed grouse using only their slingshots; they were very proficient at hitting their targets. Their little brothers and I would go along with them on the hunts near their homes, just to watch them shoot the birds with such accuracy. I was always amazed at how successful they were in getting enough birds for their families' suppers. I, on the other hand, would probably have starved if I'd had to depend on my slingshot skills. But I was learning.

Rosie and her family lived south of our property. Her house was usually my first stop of the day, if my nephews hadn't gotten to our house first. Rosie and Samuel had seventeen children, so I was never short of playmates. Rosie's yard was always abuzz with activity, as other children from the surrounding area spent a lot of time playing around her house. She was very good with children, and she enjoyed hearing their laughter as they played. This no doubt provided her with the assurance that her younger ones were safe, as they played close to her house where she could look out to check on them occasionally.

We spent most of the summer days swimming, and this activity continued late into the fall. One year when Lawrence and I were about six and Bobby was about five, the lake had started to freeze over; we discovered that my dad's barge had trapped water in it from the late fall rains. The ice on the water was only about 6 millimetres (1/4 inch) thick, so we started breaking up the ice. We took our clothes off and swam in the barge until we couldn't control the chattering of our teeth. The water in the barge was 75 centimetres (29.53 inches) deep ,and we had so much fun we probably would have done it again the following day had the ice not frozen so thick over night that we could not break it.

The fun carried on through the winter months since there were lots of steep hills we could slide down; every kid owned his or her own sled or toboggan. There was a steep hill by our house that we often used for sliding parties in the evenings. During the – 37°C (– 34.6°F) temperatures, it was nice to have a warm place nearby, like our house, when we were sliding down the hill behind our home. We were always welcome to warm up at the house nearest to whichever sliding hill we were on. We would pour hot water on the runners of the sleighs, making them very slick and increasing our speed down the hills. Some of the families that came would bring long toboggans that could accommodate several people. The more people on each toboggan the more fun, and laughter and the extra weight provided greater speed down the hill. I think back now and realize that we must have kept our moms busy keeping the water kettles hot for our use, and I don't recall one complaint from any of the mothers. I suppose they were just glad we were close to home.

My brother, George, who was ten years older than I, worked for the Canadian National Railway in another town and would often come home to visit us for two to three weeks at a time. He was very considerate. For example, when he planned to go across the lake to another store, he would come and ask me what he could bring back for me. He would spend days making toys for me in my dad's shop. One winter, he made me a tractor train set, complete with hitches for each sleigh and caboose. Tractor trains were tractors pulling four or five sleighs each, which included a caboose for the crew to sleep and eat in while they hauled supplies to the northern isolated communities where there were no roads. We made all kinds of trails in our backyard, where I spent hours playing with that tractor train set. It was probably the only toy I enjoyed more than my little toboggan. Owning the tractor train set started me dreaming of some day working on a tractor train, hauling freight to different communities in the north. These tractor trains came during the winter months, when they could travel across the muskegs and the lakes.

John enjoyed dog sledding, and he would often hitch up the two dogs from my dad's retired dog team and take my nephews and me for rides. These two dogs were the last of the nine dogs from the team my father used when he travelled throughout the north trading fur. The dogs loved the harness and were eager to run. It was always a thrill when they would start off running at full speed; then after 3 to 4 kilometres (1.86 to 2.49 miles), they would settle down to a steady pace. If John stopped to talk to someone, the dogs would rest for a couple of minutes; then they would start tugging on their harnesses and making noises, indicating that they were ready to go again. I was always amazed that the old lead dog understood my brother's every command. They used to get so excited when they saw John coming to their kennels because they were expecting him to hitch them up to the harness and go for a long run. The dogs seemed to look forward to these daily runs. When he returned from a long run with them, he would feed them and put fresh bedding down in their kennels, and then they were ready to bed down for the night. If we had a winter storm, John was not allowed to take the dogs out for a run, and the dogs would call and bark for hours, hoping John would come to them. I guess they knew that they were not going anywhere when he showed up just to feed them. Even though they were huskies, they were our family pets, and they were always very gentle with us.

Our family would gather in the living room every evening, sometimes to listen to the CBC radio news. I used to lay on the floor listing to grown-ups talk. I would always fall asleep, and John would pick me up and carry me to bed.

Bill had a little house south of our property. Bill was the older of the two clerks, and he always had breakfast at our house before opening the store for the day. I used to have breakfast with him so that I could listen to him eat. His false teeth clattered while he chewed, and this was great entertainment for me. Bill spent time teaching me to spell and pronounce words in the English language since my mother tongue was Cree, and it was the only language we spoke in the community. The only time I heard English spoken was when my dad talked with the government civil servants or the missionaries who traveled through our community. Sometimes these strangers stayed at our house on their way to other communities. The old storekeeper probably knew I would someday need to attend an English school, and it was his way of preparing me for that.

My father would often invite the two storekeepers to our house for supper on Friday evenings, as this was their last workday for the week. I remember running down the hill during the cold winter months to tell Thompson that he was invited for supper, as he would walk across the lake to go home. Sometimes I would catch him before he started to cross the lake. I was supposed to let these men know in the afternoon, but sometimes I would forget and remember at the last minute. Thompson always seemed so happy to hear that he was invited for an early supper since he probably didn't eat supper until he got home around 7:00 p.m. Thompson lived on the reservation at Oxford House, so he spoke the language of the people. Sometimes my father would tell Thompson about dinner a few days in advance so his wife could come as well. She often came early on Friday afternoons to visit in our area, so she and Thompson could both be at our house for the supper meal. These gatherings often took place when Dad was home. Thompson was a good man, and the people liked him. He often gave customers good advice on their purchases.

Chapter 12
Christmas in Oxford House

S OME OF THE PEOPLE in Oxford House told me that Christmas
was their favourite time of the winter season, for them and their
children. Full of family gatherings, Christmas was viewed as a special
time of great joy. The kids looked forward to receiving that gift they had
so often talked about around the supper table, the special foods that
would be prepared for the Christmas dinner, and all the friends popping
in just to wish them a very merry Christmas. Some of the families from
other communities would arrive to visit their extended families in our
community. There were families in our community, however, who were not
able to celebrate the Christmas season with their children. The government
had taken their children away to the residential schools down south, and
these children would not return home until school was out in June. The
parents did not have a choice when the authorities arrived to take their
children away. These children would be taught to speak and write in
English. The residential schools would change some of these people and
not always for the better. At one time, there were 132 federally supported
schools located across Canada.

The Canadian Indian residential school system was established in the
nineteenth century; it was intended to force the assimilation of the aboriginal
peoples in Canada into European-Canadian society. The purpose of the
separation of children from their families has been described as "killing the
Indian in the child." The attempt to force assimilation involved punishing

94

children for speaking their own languages or practicing their own faiths. There seemed to have been two primary objectives of the residential schools system—to remove and isolate children from the influence of their homes, families, traditions, and culture and to assimilate them into the dominant culture. The last federally run Indian residential school closed in 1996 in the province of Saskatchewan.

The government would send aircraft into the community late in August to haul the aboriginal children (status treaty Indians living on reservations) to various residential schools in southern Manitoba; they would be returned home at the end of June for the summer holidays. The government took children as young as six years old, and I am assuming that the intention was to enrol these children in the residential school system starting from the kindergarten or first-grade level. My nephews were sent away when they reached the age of seven during that first school year. The children who had only one parent were permitted to stay at home to help the one parent; they still had to attend the day schools in their community. The other children, who were non-aboriginal (Métis) and who lived in the community, went to the local day schools. The government required that all aboriginal children attend these schools, with or without the permission of the parents. Most of the community members were not happy with this, but there was nothing they could do but comply.

Some of the parents apparently refused to bring their kids to the airplanes that were sent to remove their children from the community. Sometimes, the children did not want to leave their parents, and they would miss the airplane ride intentionally, not showing up as scheduled. Once these airplanes were gone, the thought of residential school was forgotten. I was playing with some kids at the mission football field when a small airplane circled overhead then landed and pulled into the mission dock on the lake. As usual, the kids ran to see the airplane. It was always exciting to see who was coming or going, as these planes did not come to our community very often, and the mail plane usually came once a week.

I remember seeing two white men stepping off the plane and talking with the priest, who identified the two children they had come for. The men grabbed the two kids and hauled them into the airplane. The kids screamed and fought to get away, but the men were too strong. The airplane was pushed away from the dock, and it took off with those kids. Later, their parents would be told that their children had been taken to a residential school somewhere down south; there was nothing they could do to get their kids back since it was the law that each Indian child from the reserves would attend a residential school starting at grade one.

Some of the parents tried to hide their kids to prevent them from being taken away, but the police would eventually show up to arrest the parents if they did not give the children up. One way or another, the children would be taken. The government also had truant officers who could take children away from their parents without question since the officers were given much federal authority and no one could question or challenge them.

Another day, we ran to see an airplane that had landed on the lake, and a young boy who had problems learning basic skills—we assumed he had a learning disability—and did not speak or understand English was grabbed after being identified by a mission worker. The young boy was forced into the small airplane and taken to a residential school. Several weeks went by before he was returned home, when the residential school authorities realized they could not teach him. That young man was never the same after experiencing such terror at the residential school; he did not understand why the people at the residential school were so mean to him, and he did not know what they wanted from him. He would sit in one spot for long periods of time rocking back and forth and then putting out his arms and asking, "Why? Why?" as if someone was listening to him. I can imagine that his family was very worried for him.

As a child, I noticed the changes in my friends after their first year in residential school. They were very quiet and had to be encouraged to take part in our games. They had always been a little shy, but now they seemed more shy than usual. They were not the same happy children I used to know and play with, and I often asked other friends why they were now different, why they didn't seem as happy as they usually were. I never got a reply that I could understand, as it was a subject that no one wanted to talk about. These same kids who used to spend hours playing with the rest of the kids now spent more time at home doing nothing. When I asked them to tell me about their school down south, I expected to hear a lot of exciting adventures and about all the new things they'd seen and learned. I didn't hear any of that; nor did I hear about the things that we kids liked to share with one another like the new games they were taught or the new type of toys they must have seen and played with. I noticed a change in their behaviour—they were no longer interested in the things we used to do. It would be years down the road before I would hear the stories of their experiences.

The post office was a busy place in the weeks before Christmas since everyone would order his or her special gifts and clothing through the mail-order catalogues. The post office was located within the Hudson's Bay Company store, and while in the store, the people checked out the store goods that were on display behind the counters. There was no such thing as walking up to the shelves to handle the merchandise before buying; the clerk had to pick up the items off the shelves for you, as they were located across the hallway from the store counter. Most of the merchandise was beyond the shopper's reach; shopping meant looking from a distance and asking to see the product while the storekeeper observed. This was normal procedure in all the stores I entered, including my father's store.

The annual Sunday school Christmas concert was always a big event in our community. The concert was held in the United Methodist Church on a Friday night. The concert usually started at 7:00 p.m. and would carry on until 11:00 p.m. Most of the people walked to the church in the sometimes – 30°Celsius (– 22°F) temperatures. My dad was the only person who had a motorised toboggan in the community. I sometimes would go with him to pick up people from the far end of the community and bring them to the church. The toboggan's 40-horsepower Indian motorcycle engine with a three-speed transmission could pull a heavy load. I remember that the machine was made by The Four Wheel Drive Company in Kitchener, Ontario, Canada. The motor toboggan pulled a large horse toboggan that had built up sides made of rope and canvas to keep everyone warm and protect riders from the wind since we were capable of going up to 50 kph (31 mph) across the lake. We would make several of these trips, until we got everyone to the church by 7:00 p.m. The community was built along the lake shore, and the distance from some of these homes to the church was probably up to 8 kilometres (5 miles). My dad would haul most of these people home after the concert.

The church's large, decorated Christmas tree was erected near the front of the church. Lots of presents sat in piles under the tree, as when the people arrived, they would put the presents they'd brought for their neighbours or relatives under the tree. I remember one of the government civil servants receiving a large northern pike fish wrapped in Christmas paper. Apparently, this person was an avid sport fisherman. Many funny gifts were given, but all were appreciated. The large fish must have fed several of the government employees who worked in the community.

Once the children had completed their part in the concert, we would hear the sounds of thumping on the roof, and we knew Santa Claus had arrived and his reindeers' hooves had touched down on the roof. Someone must have been very brave to climb on the roof to make these noises, as this would have been a risk on the slippery roof in those temperatures. Santa would make a lot of noise ringing his bell and greeting the adults as he walked in. It always amazed me how he could know everyone by their first names. The teachers and ladies of the church would be Santa's helpers, distributing the presents to the children. This was a very exciting time for all the kids and adults. The presents were opened, and everyone shared in the joy of giving and receiving. Later, everyone would stay for refreshments and food that the church ladies had prepared. We kids always took lots of candy bags home, and everyone got a present, including the visitors. The church committees did a wonderful job of including everyone and making anyone who came a part of the festivities. As kids, we would talk about the events and excitement of that evening for days afterwards. The community became one big family of brothers and sisters that evening, and all went home very happy.

My dad or brothers made most of the Christmas presents I received, which was the reason my Christmas presents were very special to me. I would spend hours playing with these toys, and that my family had made them for me made me feel so special. The toys were made the way I had pictured them in my young mind. I guess I must have talked a blue streak for my dad or brothers to know what type of toy I wanted. One year, I let everyone know during supper that I was wishing for my very own sleigh. I often wondered why they never got tired of my talking about the things I was wishing for. As a child, my bedtime prayers were probably filled with detailed requests for the toys I was praying for. I can say with confidence that all my prayers were answered, in regard to my wants as well.

I remember getting out of bed around 2:00 a.m. one Christmas morning, just to have a peek at who was getting what for Christmas. My family had gone to bed late, and someone had left the living room light on, which was one of the reasons I'd gotten brave enough to get out of bed to have a look. I noticed the living room wood stove was still producing heat; someone must have put wood into the stove before going to bed. This made the living room that much more inviting since I normally stood by the stove in the mornings shaking from the low temperatures that crept into the house during the nights. The fragrance of the spruce tree standing in the living room added to my excitement. The colourful ribbons that Mom had put up weeks before ran from the four corners of the ceilings making an *X* in the middle. Large bell figures made out of thin red paper hung from the middle of the rooms, smaller bells hung from the top corners of the windows, and bunches of mistletoe hung over the doorways. Christmas decorations filled every nook and cranny in our dining room, living room, and kitchen. Holly and spruce decorated the outside doorways. It always felt like Christmas when all those decorations were up.

I sat there listening to the sounds of the night in our home and admiring the large bells that hung from the middle of the room. Occasionally I'd glance at the Christmas tree and its colourful decorations, which reflected the light from the lamp and the flickering light from the stove, making the ornaments look like they were dancing to a drumbeat. The fire emitted its light through the vents. The ornaments moved in a circular motion, as they were driven from the rising heated air from the stove. Dad's snoring in the bedroom competed with the crackling noise of the fire in the big wood stove. I was enjoying the sounds and smells so much that I had nearly forgotten why I had gotten out of bed. I approached the Christmas tree and noticed all the presents under the tree, and the stockings hanging along the wall were already full! *Santa must have been here already*, I thought with excitement. I saw the new toboggan that my dad had made for me. I sat on the floor admiring it and noticed the odour of fresh paint emitting from it, and I was so happy. I sat there for a long time, just touching and stroking my new toboggan, and my heart was filled with joy; I felt I must be the happiest person alive. After admiring my present for a long time, I started back to my bed, completely forgetting to look at the presents the other members of our family would receive.

I must have fallen into a deep sleep because John was shaking me to get up—it was Christmas morning, and the presents would be opened soon.

I jumped out of bed and raced for the living room to get my toboggan. Of course I received other presents, which added to my excitement, but I think the toboggan was the best present I had ever received.

Christmas Day was always a very special event in our home. Mom would start cooking our traditional Christmas dinner, which included several turkeys that Dad had ordered for the occasion. We would always have lots of leftover food to munch on in the coming days. Mom usually made the Christmas puddings, pastry, and lots of different types of cookies a few days before Christmas, and these were my favourite. There would be all kinds of cakes and cookies to snack on in the coming days. John worked at home, while George usually came home for Christmas. Norma was celebrating Christmas with her family in another town. Nellie hadn't come home since she was too far away at the school down south. Ralph was in the armed forces and was probably out of the country. Rosie and her family would be over for a while. John and George helped by keeping the manual ice-cream maker turning; the vanilla ice cream was probably my favourite homemade ice cream. They also made sure we had lots of wood to keep the stoves going and kept the water reservoir full while waiting for dinner.

The afternoon Christmas dinner was for my parents' customers and friends in the community. These people were invited over to our house for Christmas Day to thank them for their patronage for the past year. Most of these people brought their toboggans along, as many would slide down the hill by our house. My brothers, sisters, and mother would be kept busy preparing meals and keeping the wood bins and water reservoirs full. Many pots of tea, to go with the meals and to drink during after-dinner visits in our living room, were brewed.

The work was hard for Mom, who also entertained our guests and seemed to love serving. The people would often express their appreciation for being included in this festive celebration. Thinking back now, I can understand why my mom started cooking many days in advance of Christmas Day. With the many people who came for the dinner, we still had lots of food and pastry left over. Everyone had fun at the sliding party. I have many fond memories of those occasions. And everyone left happy and full. Some of the guests would take more than they could possibly eat so they could take their leftovers home, a tradition that I observed is still carried on to this day. I always thought that some of the older women from our community wore those large silk scarves so they could use the scarves to package the pastry and food they were taking home. The packaged material was then secure and easy to carry.

As I have mentioned earlier, one winter George made me a set of tractor trains that I would spend hours playing with outside in the snow. Each year, the Christmas tree produced more exciting presents than it had the year before. John or George would help me make or purchase something for my mother and dad for Christmas. My mother always helped me pick out something from the store or from the mail-order catalogue for my two brothers who would be home for Christmas. One year, I made a really nice slingshot with the help of my brothers—of course to give to a friend. I didn't have a slingshot. When it was time to wrap the gift, I began to have second thoughts that tempted me to keep the gift, as it was a nice slingshot. Then I remembered my little friend didn't have one, so I wrapped it and took it over to his place to leave under his family's Christmas tree. I was always convinced that I had to be the luckiest kid alive to belong to a loving family and to get so many wonderful presents.

Later that evening, we would go to the Christmas service at the church as a family. Refreshments were served after the service, and all the churchgoers sat around enjoying each other's company. This was called the fellowship time, and I so much enjoyed these times with all the people.

New Year's Eve celebrations were held in the community band hall. The evening activities began early in the evening, with jigging, square dancing, and the box social event. There were other games and contests for everyone, and these activities came with prizes to be won. The activities would stop at about 10:00 p.m., and dinner would be served to everyone present. This was a time when the people would visit with one another since some of the people came from other communities to celebrate Christmas and New Year's with extended family. I don't remember any other activity that took place during this one special night. There were no fireworks back then. We celebrated in this manner, with neighbours and friends. When midnight came, everyone would greet one another and wish each other the best in the new year.

D URING THE MIDDLE OF summer, the people of Oxford House would celebrate their annual Treaty Days; the celebration usually lasted for three full days. Every Indian band member would receive his or her annual treaty money in the amount of five dollars per person per year from the Department of Indian Affairs through the local Indian agent. A Royal Canadian Mounted Police officer, dressed in his scarlet dress uniform was present at this annual event.

During the Treaty Days, the federal government's Medical Services Department took the opportunity to perform annual chest X-rays, medicals, and dental checkups, which always included pulling teeth out since brushing or flossing teeth was not yet a common practice in the community. The department was able to make contact with just about everyone on their band list, as nearly everyone came to these annual treaty day celebrations. This was also when the government departments would update their records on the deaths, births, and marriages of the band members, with the aid of records kept by the church. The government set up medical tents beside the band hall, and a generator was flown in along with the X-ray equipment on a Norseman float plane to supply the electrical power. The airplane made several trips getting all the equipment into the community, which had to be set up before the Treaty Days began.

This was a very special time for the people, and the festivities offered lots of competitive games; fun games; dances; food; and most importantly, the ice cream that was flown in by aircraft for this occasion.

The people who lived far from the area would arrive with their families a couple days in advance to set up their tents, which would be their homes during the Treaty Days. The tent community was set up in a clearing by the lake near the band hall. The campers would prepare their food on the open fires, and the aroma from their cooking used to make me hungry. We would come from across the lake and stay for the full day until late into the night.

Teachers, the church committee, and the chief and council organized the daily activities, and they made sure everyone participated in the activities. The days were filled with much joy and laughter, as everyone took part, obviously enjoying the events. First, second, and third place winners of the competitive games received prizes, and, of course, one could enjoy a wide variety of food available in the concessions throughout the festivities.

My favourite memory was the ice cream, which was transported to the community by aircraft. The ice cream arrived in round cardboard containers, which were shipped in freezers that could be plugged in on arrival. A team of horses pulling a wagon would transport everything to the activity grounds. I had never seen any electrical freezers in our community; the electrical service was limited, which was why the portable electrical generator came along. The freezers were like large, long boxes with small doors at the top. The ice-cream freezers were lined up along the inside wall of the largest concession tent in plain view, making every child drool with anticipation of his or her first lick of an ice-cream cone.

As I walked by the tents, my nose would suddenly pick up an odor that would excite my taste buds, causing my mouth to water. The aroma of freshly cooked hot dogs and hamburgers emitted from the concessions and drew me away from the excitement of the competitions. I would realize I had stopped and stood silently, simply inhaling the sweet smells of food being cooked. These concessions had all my favourite foods—moose meat sandwiches, fillets of fresh fish, freshly cooked bread buns, bannock, and all kinds of pies and cakes that came with a scoop of ice cream. As much as I wanted to eat everything, I was always cautious not to get too full, as I was saving all the room for the ice cream.

The kids who took part in the races received cones as prizes, and I must have entered every race to get my share of the ice cream. When I received my vanilla ice-cream cone as a prize, I would savor every lick, hoping it would last all day. I was told that it took about fifty licks to finish off an ice-cream cone, but I know it took more than that for me to finish off my cones since I took tiny licks to make it last longer. I soon realized the taste of the commercial ice cream could not compete with Mom's homemade recipe; however, it was still ice cream, and I still couldn't get enough of it. I was always amazed at the amount of food I could take in and never gain an ounce of fat on my body. It only took about an hour before I was ready for more of this great food.

My friend Jack used to enter all the pie-eating contests, and I would go along to cheer him on. He seemed to be a slow eater and never won a pie-eating contest. I finally asked him one day why he entered these contests when he knew he could not win. His answer was that he didn't care who won as long as he got to eat some of the pie.

The constant blaring of the portable generator in the background was no match for the sounds of cheering and shouting children in the distance, as they scrambled to pick partners for the next competition that would surely yield more prizes. The adults contributed to the sounds as well. As they participated in the adult games, a lot of laughter and praise for those who did very well, especially agile seniors, filled the air. The happenings of the day would be retold over and over again, as friends recounted the events. I loved being around the adults when they took part in the sports events because it was fun to be around people who appreciated one another. I especially appreciated the way they encouraged the weaker players. I believe the individuals who took part felt appreciated upon hearing all the encouragement, even if they didn't win the competition. I know the better players would slow down a bit to let the weaker players win; I saw and felt the love these people had for one another.

The evenings were filled with activities, starting with the showing of a movie and the jigging contests. The square dancing was last, and that would last late into the night. The participants and the audience would take a break after the jigging contest to serve dinner for everyone before the square dancing began. The square dancing was my favourite dance to watch since this was an activity that included all ages. Some of the men and women were talented dancers, and it was a pleasure to watch these people perform. The men who took part in the dances wore their best moose-hide moccasins, which displayed artistic beadwork along the tops and sides. They wore the moccasins with rubbers called moccasin rubbers that were like a shoe to keep the moccasins dry when walking on wet ground. Those who took part in the dances removed these rubbers to display their fancy footwear. Some men wore moose-hide jackets that were decorated with beadwork across the chest, the upper back, and all around the lower arms. Moose-hide fringes hung along the back of the arms, as well as across the upper back and across the chest just below the beadwork. The jigging was also very exciting to watch. The young women danced with such graceful movements that they were like tops that were spun, twirling around the floor. The musicians used guitars, violins, and a tambourine or a stomper to provide the beat for the dancers. The stomper was an individual who would provide a beat by stomping his feet on the floor, keeping in time with the music. Today, drums are used for the same purpose.

The box social was a way of raising money for a good cause while providing the young unmarried people the opportunity to meet and have lunch together. These events raised money for some need in the community or for someone who was going away for medical reasons. My oldest brother, who was in the armed forces, was a recipient of a box social event. When the women heard he was leaving for Korea in the early 1950s, the community wanted to present him with a departing gift. For the box social, the single women in the community would prepare lunch boxes, which would then be displayed at the front of the hall. The young men would look over the boxes and take note of the lunch box they wanted to bid on. Every lunch box was wrapped in nicely decorated, colourful paper and ribbons and clearly marked to indentify the young lady who had prepared it. The boxes would be raffled off to the highest bidder, and sometimes two or three men would try to outbid one another to have the privilege of sharing the lunch box with its preparer. I am sure that many a young man saved his money for months in advance, hoping for the chance to share a lunch with the young lady he admired most. Most of the bidders were single men, as the tradition was they would share the box lunch with the lady who had prepared it, thus forming a relationship that would eventually end up with a proposal for marriage. I always thought that was the only purpose for these box socials, which the local ladies of the community organized. This event was also practiced in other communities. I still remember my family attending a celebration and dance in Norway House along the Jack River area where a box social similar to those organized in Oxford House was held. I was too young then to participate in those events, but I sure enjoyed observing.

The ladies of our community always seemed concerned about the single persons, especially once they'd reached their twenty-first birthday. The planning to get certain young people together was evident, even to me at that early age. I would often overhear the plots to get certain persons together. I remember some ladies even tried to get our old storekeeper, Bill, hitched up with a certain woman from across the lake. Thinking back now, I do remember seeing that woman at his house visiting him, but the pair never did get married. I guess they just ended up being good friends.

One of my brothers was a victim of such a plot; the local matchmakers intended to unite him with one of the local ladies, and I think he messed up by not going along with that relationship since the woman in question was a very pretty and resourceful woman who was well liked by the people of the community.

The chief, George Colon, made himself available at all the functions, wearing his official chief's uniform, which consisted of a dark suit with a colourful sash around his waist. He was a very important man whom the people appreciated and respected.

The Treaty Days was an exciting event for the young people too, as it was geared for the whole family. With all this excitement, no one concerned him or herself with the medical people on the grounds doing their work. When it was time for someone to see a doctor or get an X-ray, he or she complied without hesitation and with lots of cooperation so as to get back to the activities without too much delay. Normally, everyone tried to avoid these professionals.

It was always sad to see these activities come to a close. I am sure many of the people forgot their problems for a few days, as they took part in the joy and laughter that Treaty Days brought. For those who travelled great distances to take part in the festivities, the end of the festival meant that it was time to say good-bye to their many friends and break camp for the trip home.

All the medical equipment, generators, and tents would be dismantled, and the airplane would begin hauling the medical equipment to the next destination. Oxford House would return to the tranquil community we loved.

The day after the Treaty Days celebrations ended was probably the saddest day of the year. It seemed like an eternity before those fun-filled days would return. For me, it took a couple of days before I got back to my normal routine and realized there were lots of adventures to look forward to.

Tents and tepees used during Treaty Days.

Chapter 14
Evil That Lurks in the Shadows

ONE BENEFIT OF LIVING in a small, northern community in late 1949 was that you were able to experience drinking the cool, clean, and natural clear water from our beautiful lakes. There was no need to filter or purify the water that we drank. Likewise, the air we breathed was clean and fresh since the industries that pollute the environment did not yet exist. Those of us who lived in the land of plenty often took for granted the bountiful fish in our lakes and the game animals that populated our forests. The neighbours were good, always sharing their prizes from a successful hunt or fishing trip. Everyone shared the joys of living in this great northland, and the happiness was evident in the sound of the laughter from everyone, especially the children, who had not yet experienced the concerns of tomorrow or the worry for one's own safety in this paradise. But somewhere in this paradise evil always lurked, evil that was ready to pounce on the vulnerable and the weak—usually innocent children were the chosen victims.

As a child, I personally experienced some of this evil that I am about to talk about. I knew that as I wrote these memories on paper, I would stop to break down and weep because the pain in reliving these events cuts as deeply now as it did then. I was aware that God did not always remove the memories of events that took place in our lives, even if reliving them brought pain. The scars of sins we commit or sins that were committed against us would never be erased, for they were forever etched on our hearts. God would save us, forgive us, and change us if we asked Him, but the scars from sin would always be on our hearts. I also realized that I needed to expose the pain in my heart in order for God to apply His healing completely and establish that relationship I desired with Him. After all, He was aware of all that I had been through, and He would make the wrongs I'd suffered right in the end.

There were times I was negligent in my childhood for not knowing and recognizing the wrongs that were done in my presence. I think back now, and if only I could go back and do it again, I would speak up for or get help for those in need of protection.

I have not used names of the individuals involved, since I understand their families may wish to take these awful experiences to their graves, as I had once intended to do.

Initially, my plan to write my childhood story did not include this part of my life. Friends who have listened to my stories have often asked if there were any negative experiences in my childhood. My answer was always the same—that I never dwell on them. So it was at their urging and encouragement that I included this part, as a way of expressing my complete healing and as a way of encouraging and supporting those living in small, isolated communities who have been wounded and abused. I urge those who have gone through similar experiences not to keep them hidden with the hope of taking the secret of these wounds to the grave, as doing so will rob you of the joys of living; a secret like this is like a sore that continues to fester and grow, for it does not heal until it is confronted and turned over to our Creator, who can heal the wounded heart and mind. You must forgive those who abused you, for an unforgiving spirit will have consequences in your life.

Also, now that my parents have passed on, I am free to express myself, knowing that what I say now will not bring them heartache, pain, guilt, and remorse of knowing what really took place during that summer when I suddenly became very sick. I always felt it would have been too much for them to know the truth about why I became so sick during that one hot, summer day. I wanted to protect them from harm because of a threat I had received. Even after many years had passed, I used to awaken in the middle of the night drenched in perspiration from dreaming about and reliving those awful moments. There were times when I needed to find a quiet place where no one would see or hear me weeping since I could not control the emotions that welled up inside of me; I would sob quietly in a private place where I could be all alone. It was during these times that I felt God's presence near me, and I knew He understood me and loved me. I was always strengthened after our time together. He truly is a comforter, and He was the only one with whom I shared this bad experience until now. I know people can talk over their experiences with one another in the hope they will forget, but ultimately, it is only our Creator who can bring the true and lasting healing.

Initially, I had kept these events secret from my parents for fear that my abuser would carry out his threat and hurt my family. After I heard that my abuser had died, I realized then that I was not able to talk about it since I felt too ashamed of what had happened. My only comfort was the knowledge that God loved me and cared for me, which prevented me from losing my mind.

I knew everyone on my side of the community, and it was not unusual for me to be seen playing with the other children at their homes or along the lake shore 4.8 kilometres (3 miles) from my home. Likewise, those children would come to play on our side of the community. I sometimes went along with other kids and their dads to check their rabbit snares or just out hunting grouse for the afternoon. I always felt at home in many of my friend's homes, and their parents treated me like I was one of their kids. We often played baseball or soccer in someone's yard, and the families would provide refreshments for everyone. Some of these people carried their water up a steep hill, sometimes up to .8 kilometres (.5 miles) to their house, and the families freely shared the water, without complaints from the older brothers who had to carry the water.

On a beautiful, warm day, shortly after I had celebrated my sixth birthday, another boy my age and I had gone to a schoolyard across the lake to play. The school was out for the summer, and other kids were playing in the schoolyard on the teeter-totters. Later in the afternoon, the two men working on the schoolyard informed us that it was getting late in the day and that we should be going home, as they also were leaving for the day. My friend and I decided to walk along the beach on our way home. A road ran along the lake shore in the forest, and a thick growth of spruce trees lined each side of the road. We decided that it was more fun to be running and playing in the sand as we travelled home.

At one point, we took our shoes off and walked in the water, chasing small minnows along the shallow part of the beach while carrying our shoes under our arms. The clean, white sand felt good on our feet, and the fine grains of sand would push up between our toes, tickling our feet, which made us laugh that much more. The water felt very warm, and we squinted from the brightness of the sunlight reflecting off the white, sandy bottom. Sometimes, we would stand still and watch the sunbeams dancing in the water and the little minnows moving about as if they were being chased by the sunbeam's movements. We would squeal with joy when we watched the perch swim close to our feet as if they were not aware of our presence. As usual, we took our time getting home, playing all along the way in this manner.

We were approaching the Catholic mission, where we planned to stop and visit the brother and the priest; we were always welcomed at the mission. We'd come to the end of the beach and had stopped to put on our shoes when a young man from across the lake approached us. We knew his family very well, and everyone liked his mom and dad; I had often played with his younger brother and sisters, who were near my age. He told us he'd found some baby birds in a nest, and he wanted to know if we wanted to see them.

Of course we wanted to see the baby birds! We were very excited to hear of his discovery. He said it was a long ways into the forest, but we didn't care, as long as we got to see the tiny birds and maybe even hold them. He took the lead, and we followed along, talking a mile a minute and never questioning him as we went deeper into the forest. At one point, I was aware that we were not following a trail, and I asked how we were going to find our way back to the beach. He assured us that he would bring us back to where he'd found us, and with that, we marched on. We walked until my friend complained he was getting tired, and that is when the young man told us that we had to be quiet and we could see the birds one at a time so as not to disturb them. My friend wanted to see the birds first, and the young man told me to wait there until it was my turn.

The man and my friend had been gone for a while when I heard the two of them approaching the spot where I waited. My friend was crying. I asked him what had happened, and he did not say anything to me. I noticed his face was swelling and there was blood on it, and the young man told me my friend had fallen off a tree and that he would wait here for us, as it was my turn to see the birds. At that point, I noted a change in his voice, as if he had become impatient with us; he seemed to display a sense of anger towards us. When I saw my friend acting so hysterical, I told him we wanted to go home now, as I had to take my friend home. When I told him that, he threatened to leave us there and told us we could find our way back by ourselves. At that point, I began to panic. I knew I would get lost in the forest, as I didn't know my way out of this place; it was getting late in the day, and soon it would be dark. I agreed to go along with him to see the birds, as he promised it would not take long.

I turned to my crying friend. I told him we would hurry back, and then we left. I was beginning to get scared because of the change in the young man's attitude towards us, and I really didn't want to see the birds anymore. But I was also afraid he would leave us there, and I didn't know our way back to the beach.

We walked quickly for a while, and I remember approaching some large boulders standing in a large circle. When we were inside the circle of boulders he stopped, turned, and became very mean towards me. When I refused to do as he instructed, he struck me and knocked me down to the ground. Once I received the beating, I became very scared. My assailant told me he was going to leave me and my friend there unless I did what I was told. I finally obeyed, and he did things to me that caused me to experience such excruciating pain that I thought I would pass out. I would have mental scars for the rest of my life. I didn't know how long we were there. I was unable to stand up as a result of the pain I was experiencing.

Later, my abuser helped me get dressed and half-carried me out to where my friend was laying on the ground, crying and in pain. By now, dark bruises were showing on my friend's face, and the blood had begun to dry. I did not have any bruises on my face like my friend did, and the young man told us that if we ever told anyone what had happened, he would hurt us and our families very badly, and that we had better keep this to ourselves. He took us back to the road and disappeared back into the forest.

My friend and I walked back to the beach to wash ourselves; we washed over and over again, as if we could wash the experience from our lives. We couldn't stop trembling, as fear had overtaken us; we were simply overwhelmed with fear and shame. We had gotten very dirty from being in the bush, and my friend's swollen face was bleeding around his eyes and ears. We washed the best we could in silence, but we were still very afraid and didn't want to go home like this. For a while, we didn't know what to do, so we just stayed by the water. We agreed that we would never tell our families, as we didn't doubt that the young man would come and harm them as he had threatened to do if we told.

We went to my friend's home first, and when his mother saw him, she let out a shriek that caused me to tremble with fear, as I thought she was angry with us. She was crying hysterically; she tried talking to her son between sobs when she could catch her breath. She kept asking him how he had gotten all those bruises, but we were too scared to talk, and like me, he just shook with fear. I can still remember the horrified look on her face, as she tried to talk to us to ascertain what had happened. Her voice sounded like she was screaming at us, and the shrieks she uttered scared us all the more. She could not control her voice because of the horror she was seeing, and we were both too scared to say anything. She went hysterical when we couldn't respond to her questions, and I was shaking like a leaf. When she sat down and gave us a few minutes, my friend told her we were climbing trees and he had fallen down onto a pile of rocks. I was still terrified at this point. After my friend's mother dressed his wounds, she cleaned my face and removed the mud from my clothes. His older brother walked me home without saying anything to me all the way home, which made me wonder if he knew the truth. I was very afraid and concerned.

I wondered what I was going to say when I got home since I was still trembling with fear and feeling ashamed in every part of my being. My mother had my supper waiting when I arrived home, and she was busy in the kitchen doing some last-minute baking for the following day. I attempted to eat, but I couldn't keep any food down. I told her I was not feeling well and I was going to bed. She asked me how I was feeling and if I had eaten anything that might have upset me. I don't even know how I replied. She must have thought I was really sick, as I usually stayed up until I fell asleep in the living room. I needed to be alone; I felt sick with guilt and fear.

My mother woke me up late that night to tell me I was bleeding and asked if I was hurt. She had seen the blood on my sheets when she came to tuck me in for the night. She looked very worried, and she told me she was going to get my dad to check me over. I became very afraid, for he might ask me what happened, and I had promised my friend that we would never tell our parents. I didn't know what I was going to say.

My dad came to my bedside, and both he and Mom checked me over. Then he left to get the nurse from the nursing station, while my mother cleaned me and changed the sheets on my bed; they were soaked with my blood.

Dad was back sooner than I'd expected, and the nurse checked me for broken bones and asked me a lot of questions. She left later and promised to be back the following morning. I went back to bed wearing a diaper my mother had made from old sheets. The blood from my body continued to flow for two days, and I stayed in bed during that time. The nurse came often, and she didn't have a clue why I was losing so much blood. She put me on a special diet and told me not to eat anything else.

I never told my parents or the nurse what had happened to me that day, and they didn't ask me any more questions. Once the blood flow stopped, I still had to go once in a while to see the nurse. The nurse and my father talked about possibly sending me out to see a doctor. By then, the bleeding had stopped, and they decided she would keep checking on my condition. My mother told me later that she went without sleep during those two days while she kept watch over me.

I often wondered if they ever considered what had happened to me, as sexual assault was a crime that was unheard of in those days. The local people of our community probably thought that the type of people who did harm to children did not exist in our God-fearing community. My parents must have thought that I would tell them if someone had punched me in the stomach to cause all that internal bleeding.

A few days after the assault, I came home from playing with the neighbourhood children and saw the bloody sheets flapping on the clothesline. My mother had attempted to wash the bloodstains off my sheets, but she had not been able to. When I saw the bloody sheets, I felt the same fear arise within me that I had felt the day that the young man abused us. I started to tremble, and I had to go and sit by the lake shore until my crying and trembling had stopped. I felt anger and hate rise within me for that young man; I began thinking that someday I would destroy him. Had my mother seen me lose control of my emotions, I might have been tempted to tell her the truth, to ease the pain in my heart, but fortunately, she was in the house at the time and had not seen me approaching.

I never saw my friend again, as he remained secluded at home and was later sent away to a residential school at a very young age. My heart goes out to his mother, who must have been heartbroken when the authorities took her little boy, whom she loved so much. I had watched so many mothers weep for their children at the docks when they had to say good-bye to their little ones who were being taken away to schools.

I never again saw the young man who'd abused us. I made sure I didn't go to his side of the lake again without an adult companion. I often wondered if his actions were the result of the abuse he had received at one of those residential schools, which he'd attended as a child. I heard he died on his trapline a few years later as a result of an accident. I can only imagine the guilt and shame he must have experienced during those last few months on this earth. I forgave him for what he did to me a long time ago while I was still a child. My parents taught me to always forgive those who did me wrong; otherwise, the resentment we harbour would be like a poison that grinds away at our conscious. Forgiving this abuser was one of the hardest things I have done, and it has brought me healing and peace of mind.

As long as we are in this world, there will always be someone with an evil intent in his or her heart, and we can only hope these people get help before it overtakes them, as it did the man who abused my friend and me. The Bible teaches us that each one of us is tempted when we are carried away and enticed by our own lust. Then when lust has conceived, it gives birth to sin; and when sin is accomplished, it brings forth death (James 1:14–15).

The young and the innocent are often victimized by evil that crosses their paths. Had it not been for my faith in a loving God and a wonderful family, I probably would have gone insane before reaching my teen years. When I left this problem at the altar of my God and asked for the strength to forgive this man, I began to experience joy returning to me. I have never looked back, as I never wanted to take back what I had left at the altar that day. And the Lord has been faithful in helping me. I don't have bad feelings about the experience; as I have said, I left it all at the altar, and it will always remain there.

Had I carried a grudge and allowed the anger and hate to fester, it would have destroyed me by now. The memory and pain of that ordeal will always be there, but the anger, hate, and shame are gone. I believe God has taken away those things that could have eventually destroyed me. I often think back to my childhood, when my parents taught me to always forgive those who did me wrong and to never hold a grudge. We can always take our problems to the Lord and leave them there; otherwise, they will destroy us.

Years later, I would learn that I was not the only person to have gone through such a hellish experience. As I reached my teen years, I would listen to individuals I'd gotten to know whose trust I'd earned as a friend. It was hard to listen to their stories as the pain, shame, and fear that they were feeling also surfaced in my being. These friends were very shy, and it took a lot of courage, strength, trust, and patience to reveal those events that they may never have told their parents or families. I will never retell their stories; nor will anyone else. And their secrets will go to their graves with them to wait eternity's fate. Among the people I grew up with, talking about these kinds of sin is taboo, as it brings too much pain and shame to the victims, who must relive those experiences each time they are revealed. The victims prefer to never repeat their stories. We have one thing in common that we often reassure each other with, and that is that God is faithful and loves us in spite of this shame and our experience will not stand in the way of His love for us. I can only imagine the shame and regret that awaits the abusers when, one day, they stand before our Creator, who is the judge of all the earth. I would not hesitate to beg for their mercy, knowing the end result of their guilt if they never repented for their crime.

Even though bad things happened, as they do, I knew at some point I must start to live again, as the future was still before me. I would learn to trust again, enjoy being alive, and be happy.

As children in our community, we travelled many kilometres in a day, running the length of our side of the community and exploring the unknown areas. We would meet or overtake people walking along the bush paths within the community since there were no roads at the time. So if anyone knew of a shortcut to a destination, it soon became a main travel way. Many paths snaked throughout the community. If one could observe these roads from above, one could establish a shorter route by eliminating the turns and curves that went with the lake shoreline. We established shortcuts through the bush that did just that. When new, the trails were only as wide as a beaten path, so the undergrowth bush was always brushing against one's shoulders. They were like the trails that animals established by continuous travel. To make them wider, one would need to clear the brush along these pathways using an axe. One could chose several paths that eventually led to the same destination, each of which was so narrow that you had to step off the path to permit someone coming from the other direction to pass. About five routes connected the southern part of our community along the same shoreline to my father's store.

One day, my friends and I were going to a friend's house to play baseball, and we were running down one of these bush trails when we came upon a man holding a young woman. We stopped to look at them, and the girl told us to go and get her some help as she was trying to get free of this man. The man told us it was a game they were playing and that everything was okay. We must have believed the young man, and the girl didn't look frightened, so we left and continued on to our destination. We never considered what the young man and woman were doing and what possible consequences there would be for the girl if a crime was being committed; we never even thought anyone could do wrong in that God-fearing community.

I think back now, having been abused myself, and I realize I may have been able to prevent these kinds of crimes that were being done to other people, had I known and recognized them in my early age. These realizations and memories bring sorrow and grief to my heart, as I see now that, in my foolishness, I may have turned my back on someone who needed my help. Today's parents need to inform their children that there are foolish people out there who would cause others harm in order to satisfy their pleasures and lust. The perfect world I thought I was living in turned out to be quite the opposite; men and women everywhere will yield to their evil thoughts and desires and eventually commit crimes to satisfy their lust.

A policeman patrolled in our community of Oxford House only once or twice a year since there were no crimes being committed that we knew of. I saw pictures of the policeman and his dog team in my parents' photo album. The photographs had been taken during his winter patrols to our area and to other communities in the north. Other than these brief visits, he came by airplane to our community if he was needed.

When I was about eight years old, I witnessed a policeman taking away one of the men from our community. My mother told me that the arrested man had committed a crime and was being removed from the community to be punished. I think this was when I starting developing a fear of the policeman, who could take you away if you did anything wrong. I was very careful never to do anything unlawful.

A policeman who had been visiting the Methodist minister at the Oxford House Church came out of the building the same time Dad and I were leaving the game warden's home next door, where we had been visiting. My dad stopped to talk to the policeman, and he seemed very friendly. He and Dad shared a few laughs when they told each other some funny stories. The policeman was very interested in my dad's motor toboggan, so they talked about the machine and how fast one could get around using one of these. Having the policeman stand so close to me made me very nervous since this was a man my mother had told me could take people away to be punished.

I later developed a respect for these policemen since they travelled throughout the North during the long, hot, mosquito-infested summers and during the extreme cold temperatures that the winter always brought to keep our northern communities safe and peaceful. These policemen often travelled with an interpreter to the northern communities, and I am sure their presence alone prevented crime from happening.

The point of land where my father had his warehouse in Norway House was just across a small bay from the police station and jail that served northern Manitoba. The policemen who were stationed there would travel throughout the north on routine patrols or responding to the needs of the surrounding communities. It was here that I first experienced my fear of being locked up in a jail. A man who had become mentally unstable was brought in from the north. My dad came home before lunch that day with an urgent concern, and he told Mom that they needed to talk. I remember waiting with my mom as she held me close. She always held me close when she was anxious and fearful, so I knew something was about to take place. My dad had stopped to wash his hands in the kitchen while we waited in the living room area. I noticed a very concerned look on his face when he told

Mom that a dangerous man was being held at the jail in the police station next door. The policeman had informed Dad that he was holding a man who'd been flown in from the north; he said the man would be making a lot of noise during the night, which we would be hearing since we lived a short distance from the jail. A doctor had injected the man with a drug that made him sleep during the transport to the police station. This man apparently saw demons and strange creatures that tormented him during the night, so the doctor came each evening before the sun went down and gave the man a drug injection that would help him sleep.

That first night my dad had his rifle beside his bed, so I knew the situation was serious. We could hear the man screaming and crying that night after the effect of the drug wore off; the noise he made banging something against the jail walls also terrified us. I can still hear that noise when I go back into my memory and listen to that man expressing his terror at the top of his lungs. I remember the fear in his voice as he begged to be left alone. Each night during the commotion, my mother would talk loudly, telling me stories to try to drown out the noises until I fell asleep from sheer exhaustion.

I would wake up each morning with a start, only to hear the sounds of birds singing outside. During the daylight hours, the jailed man would be quiet and was probably sleeping. This went on for a couple of days, and then Dad told Mom that the man was going to be taken away to a hospital in Winnipeg the next day, weather permitting, since he was being flown out by aircraft.

My mother and I sat on the shore and watched a Norseman aircraft on the water as it taxied up to the police dock. The tormented man was strapped to a stretcher as the doctor had put him to sleep for the trip. I remember my mother saying how thankful she was that the man would finally receive medical help wherever he was being taken. I am sure she slept well that night, as she had been staying up late into the night keeping my mind occupied. I can imagine the policeman was also relieved to have that person removed from his jail. We never heard anymore about that man, as we didn't know who he was or what illness he had. I think back now and realize how fortunate we were to have lived in communities where people loved their neighbours. I have learned that the presence of evil is always near, even at the door to our heart, and when it is allowed to enter into the heart of an individual, it will produce fear that may destroy us emotionally and spiritually.

I don't have any regrets regarding my past, as I have learned to appreciate the events and circumstances God has allowed to be placed on the path of my life's journey. Looking back now, I realize He has faithfully guarded my life. In addition to my accident, my life could have ended seven times if it weren't for God's protection. I never considered those eight incidents as miracles, only the result of God's faithfulness in protecting me. I am so happy to know He loves me and that I have experienced His favour upon my life.

Chapter 15
The Tractor Trains

O NCE THE CHRISTMAS SEASON was over, there was another exciting event to look forward to—the annual arrival of the tractor trains, sometimes called cat swings. Finishing their long journeys over the frozen terrain, the cat swings arrived with the much-needed supplies. They delivered freight for the stores, health services, and construction sites. The schools also received their yearly supply of freight, including boxes of cookies that were given to school-aged children as a dietary supplement. The cookies were supposedly loaded with vitamins required for daily nourishment. The teachers handed out the cookies, and we were each supposed to eat our cookie in class in the presence of the teacher. This was the only way to make sure we ate the cookie, as it tasted awful and was very hard and chewy. This was not all. We had to go to the nursing station daily to receive our tablespoon of cod liver oil. *Now wasn't that a treat!*

The tractor trains had been around since the 1920s. They consisted of two crawler tractors, each one pulling four large freight sleighs with decks that were three feet off the ground on struts attached to ski-shaped runners. Each sleigh was capable of carrying forty-four drums of fuel or 14 tons of freight. When a train was hauling bulk fuel only, each sleigh would carry a five-thousand-gallon tank that would be pumped into storage tanks at the delivery sites. One caboose housed the crew; the caboose had a kitchen, eating area, and sleeping area. The crew ate and slept on the go in the crew caboose since these trains ran twenty-four hours a day. The crews worked six hours on and six hours off continuously during the four-month hauling season without a day off. Sometimes, heated cabooses were used for hauling the perishables.

One sleigh carried the spare parts and the diesel fuel for the tractors. This sleigh was usually hooked up next to the crew caboose, which was always at the rear of the train. Each tractor train consisted of two trains having of one cook, one brakeman, and four tractor operators. The brakeman's job was to help when coupling or uncoupling the sleighs; he had to hold the V pole (coupler) up while the tractor or another sleigh was backing up to make the coupling. He helped the operators during the shift changes, inspecting the sleighs for damage or worn parts and making sure loads were secure.

The first tractor train that went out would not carry freight since its only job was to break the trail, test the ice thickness, and build winter bridges over the creeks. The train would continue to break the road to the furthest point then return to home base to start hauling freight. The lead tractor was equipped with a dozer blade to plough the road, leaving about one foot of snow on the trail to be packed.

The tractors were fuelled and checked over during shift changes, and this would give the operators coming on shift a quiet time to eat instead of trying to eat in a rocking caboose. The trails were usually rough, and one needed to hang on with one hand while eating or sleeping. It was sort of like being rocked to sleep in a cradle, only a lot rougher, as if a cranky sister was rocking her baby sister, who did not want to go to sleep. I have always been amazed that one could sleep peacefully when the caboose was bouncing and rocking. There were times when the swing crews breaking trail and travelling on uneven ground would accidently roll the caboose on its side. It must have been a rude awakening for anyone sleeping when this happened. Usually the caboose was pulled back upright, and after a few laughs, the train continued on. The kitchen stove had a metal railing around the top to keep the pots or kettles from sliding off during the movement, as the kitchen caboose would rock going over rough ground. I was always amazed that the cooks on these trains could cook and bake on the run. Having worked on these trains, I know the food these guys prepared was delicious. The only time the rides were smooth was during the lake crossings.

Once the trains reached their destinations, the entire crew would stay awake to unload the freight, with help from the local people, whom the receiver would employ. Once the freight was unloaded, the freight going south was loaded for the journey back to home base, usually a railroad town. Sometimes a crew would miss its turn to sleep because of the time it took to load or unload the freight. I never heard any of the crewmembers complain about losing their rest time, as they realized the season was short; everyone seemed to focus on getting the much-needed materials delivered. Eventually, the other shift would be in the same situation.

This was a place where a real team spirit was practiced. Sometimes when one person was feeling ill, his cross shift would work the extra hours, permitting the sick crewmember to get a few extra hours of sleep. The comradeship was very real since everyone had the same goals. I would later work as a crewmember on one of those tractor trains, and it was during times like these that we realized how effective we could be when we worked together with one goal in mind, which made us feel that we could overcome any obstacle.

The tractor trains would encounter terrible storms and blizzards so bad that the operators could see only a few feet ahead of the tractor. They never stopped for weather. The only time the tractor trains would stop on the trail was when one of the tractors broke down or fell through the ice and sunk. Most of the time, the tractor operator would be able to jump clear of the open hole before his machine disappeared into the dark, deep waters. The sleighs being pulled did not always fall through the ice when the tractor sank; they could be pulled to safety, away from the thin ice. Every attempt would be made to rescue the sunken machine.

During my time with the tractor train crews, I lost a couple of friends, who went through the ice with their tractors. They were immediately swept under the ice by the swift currents. Usually, the bodies of the lost souls would not be recovered until spring, when the ice had cleared.

The transport companies that owned these tractor trains were all privately owned. They all bid on the freight haul contracts during the summer months so that they had plenty of time to prepare their equipment and crews for when the winter season arrived. The transport companies would bid and sign contracts to haul freight for the Canadian provincial and federal governments as the transport companies were not run by a government program. These companies also contracted out to haul freight for the stores, mining companies, and logging companies. Any private citizen could hire the trains as well to haul materials and goods at a fixed rate, usually set per kilogram (or pound). Many private citizens used these services to haul in a new boat or new furniture they had purchased from the southern stores.

As a child in our community, I was very excited when the tractor trains came to our village, as I enjoyed riding on the sleighs being pulled by those fast, powerful tractors. The only time I got to ride on the sleighs was when they delivered freight to my dad's store since I was not allowed to go too far from home during the winter months. I remember standing on a hill by our home watching the tractors shunt their sleighs around the field in preparation for delivery. They were delivering their loads to the Health Services Station and to the schools across the lake from our home. My mother must have felt sorry for me, as she let me use her prized binoculars to observe from my location; I'd watch the kids running from one sleigh to another to catch rides as the sleighs were being moved around by the tractor. Their screams of joy and laughter echoed above the sound of the machines.

Once the tractor trains unloaded their freight at my dad's store, they would haul wood for him from the south shore of the lake, which was several kilometres from our house. My father had the wood cut during the summer months, and the tractor trains would haul this wood to our place. These trains would make a couple of trips, as there were several buildings to heat during the long winters. It was during one of these trips that I had a chance to sneak onto the sleighs with a few other kids to ride out and then walk back. It was a very cold day, and the tractors were travelling at a good speed across the lake since they were empty. I am guessing when I say the temperatures were about – 30°C (– 22°F) to – 34°C (– 22°F), as those were the average winter temperatures in our area. A friend and I were the last to jump off and walk back to the village. We watched the tractor train continue travelling towards the south shore to get its load. We stood there for a while in the middle of the lake, watching and listening to the sounds of the tractors fading into the distance.

We were about 8 kilometres (5 miles) from home when we started walking towards our village in that deep, soft snow. We walked, trying to avoid stepping onto the sleigh runner tracks since they formed a slippery, icy surface from the weight of the sleighs and the friction the runners created as they moved through the snow. I had made the mistake of stepping onto one a few days before. Fortunately, it only caused me to slip and fall, landing on my back without being harmed. But the potential for one to be injured was always there, and this would not be a good place for an injury to occur.

The last time we looked back, we could see the two tractors' exhausts and the smoke from the caboose kitchen stove rising high on the horizon. We realized that we were getting cold, so we picked up the pace to keep warm. At the same time, we noticed the sky was clouding over very quickly. About this time, the wind speed picked up, and we hurried on as we had only gone about 3 kilometres (1.86 miles). We went another 2 kilometres (1.24 miles). We knew that we were not making good time, and it was getting late in the day; we were getting worried and very cold. Later on, the wind started to blow hard, swirling the snow and covering the tractor train tracks in front of us. We were so cold that we could barely understand each other as our mouths and lips were very stiff. My friend was the first to be able to see his house, and he asked if I wanted to stop to warm up, which I should have done.

We then parted, as he headed towards the shore slowly, barely able to walk against the blowing wind. I had about 2 kilometres (1.24 miles) to go to get to get home. By the time I could see my parents' house, I was approaching the lake shore in the storm that had quickly developed; I was crawling on my knees since my feet were so cold I'd lost feeling in them and I was not able to stand on them because they were frozen. I finally got to the house. My mom had been looking for me, as it was now starting to get dark. I remember my feet starting to hurt when I was in the warm room.

Mom got the tub out and filled it with ice and cold water for me to soak my feet in. I didn't want to put my feet into the cold, icy water since I was already cold. My mother knew how to be convincing, and somehow I ended up with my feet soaking in that ice water. I don't have to mention how concerned she was for me. Someone had gone to get the nurse, and she arrived to help Mom. I don't know exactly how long I was in that water, but it was several hours, and when the feeling started to come back, the pain was unbearable. The pain was so great I begged Mom to use warm water instead, and she wouldn't. She eventually removed some of the ice from the water when the colour of my skin started to return, and the water started to feel warmer even though it was still cold.

Later on, as I grew older, I was able to talk to her about that day; she explained that she could not remove the ice from the water until my feet started showing some colour, indicating blood circulation. As an example of what would have happened if she'd used warm water instead of cold water and ice, she took a frozen whitefish out of the icebox and put it in a pan. As she explained that this was what would have happened if she had heeded to my begging for warm water, she poured warm water into the pan of frozen fish. I watched as the fish flesh fell apart in the warm water. She explained that warm water would have destroyed my flesh like it did this fish. Then she took another fish and dipped it into ice water. It stayed together and gradually thawed.

I often thought of that illustration and wondered what I would have done if one of my children was screaming in pain and begging me to change my course of action. Would I have given in to my child's pleading rather than doing the right thing? As parents, it sometimes takes great pain to maintain our course of action for the benefit of our children.

While the experience helped me develop an awe of nature's immense power, it did not change my mind about the tractor trains. From the time my brother George made me a tractor train set I was hooked! I spent many cold days outside playing with those toy tractor trains. I often dreamed of someday working on a real tractor train. Recalling those days now, I realize that my dream came true. Those were the best years of my life, as working on those trains was pure joy.

The first time I decided to go to Ilford, Manitoba, to look for work on the tractor trains, I had five dollars on me. I knew one man from our village who worked for one of the privately owned tractor train companies based out of Ilford, so I went to see him for advice. I was fifteen years old when I started working on the trains. I was still going to school when I got the idea that maybe someone would hire me and train me on those tractor trains. It was very cold that winter, but I wasn't worried as to where I would sleep since I couldn't afford a hotel room anyway. I did have a sleeping bag and warm clothes with me, so I could always make camp and sleep in the bush beside a warm fire. I had brought a few sandwiches that would last me for two days.

The train arrived at Ilford around 10:00 p.m., and I had purchased a return train fare in case I failed to secure employment. The returning train would arrive in two days, so I had time to look for a job. My friend worked for Lindal Transport, which operated a couple of tractor trains out of Ilford. Lindal Transport had hauled freight for my dad, so I was hoping Mr. Lindal might hire me and train me. When I met Mr. Lindal, he immediately inquired as to where I was staying for the night. When I told him I didn't have a place to sleep yet, he told me I could stay in the bunkhouse until I found a job or returned home. Lindal Transport was not able to hire me that day, as the same people worked for the company each year. I helped Mr. Lindal's men load sleighs, with the intention of paying for my keep as Mr. Lindal had refused to accept my five-dollar bill for payment for my room and board.

Mr. Lindal talked to the owner of Johnson's Transport, and he agreed to see me. The interview was scheduled for the next morning with the owner, Mr. Johnson. Mr. Johnson did most of the talking during the interview, and I was just hoping he would hire me. He must have received a good report from Mr. Lindal, as he mentioned that I was appreciated for all the work I had done at Mr. Lindal's yard loading sleighs. He also must have known I would work hard if I got hired. Finally, he asked me if I could start work the next morning, and so I moved into one of the warm cabooses that day. I don't know if I slept that night as I was so excited to finally have the opportunity to be on a tractor train. I worked around the yard helping load sleighs. I also had the opportunity to practice running the tractors during this time, and I caught on quickly. When it was time for me to be put on a swing crew, I was told I would take the train to Gilliam and drive one of the tractors there that was hauling fuel to the Mid-Canada Radar Sites.

That winter we hauled fuel to the Mid-Canada Radar Line. Mr. Johnson must have liked me since he offered me employment during the summer months. I made sure he got his money's worth each time I worked for him to show my appreciation. The second year I worked for Sigfusson Transport, which hauled the majority of the freight for the communities that year.

The tractor train crews inspected their equipment at the beginning of January, making sure the required repairs were done and that any modifications needed were completed. Sometimes the sleighs needed modifications to accommodate the special loads they would be hauling.

There was a lot of shuttling of sleighs around the shop yard to get the sleighs loaded.

When the people living in the northern communities heard the tractors or saw the lights from the tractor trains approaching far in the distance, they would walk or run out to meet them to have the opportunity to ride on the sleighs. Oxford House reserve was situated on high ground so the community could see the lights from the tractors crossing White Mud Lake, several kilometres away. This gave the people ample time to walk far enough out of the community to get a long ride back. The very young were always a problem since they did not realize the dangers associated with these powerful machines. The local community constables would try their hardest to keep the kids off the sleighs, but the efforts were futile, as there were just too many children trying to jump onto the sleighs at once. The constables used to threaten the kids with willow sticks, with permission of course from the local chief and council acting on behalf of all the parents. All the threats and the willow-swinging did not discourage the young riders, and it was a real safety concern for us. The most important thing to these young people was to get a ride on these tractor trains. Some of the adults were just as bad as the kids. I once saw an elderly lady running alongside the sleighs trying to jump on to get a ride back into the community. I had to stop to let her on, as she was losing ground and struggling in the soft, deep snow. I often stopped my train to allow everyone to get on the sleighs since I thought they would be safer once they all sat down and enjoyed the ride. I soon realized that such was not the case, as they would jump off and onto the next sleigh, sometimes racing with one another to be the first to get to the next sleigh or the next train behind me. They would also jump onto the hitches between the sleighs we called V poles, which coupled the sleighs together, and disappear out of sight as they crouched down low under the sleigh while we were travelling. We also tried stopping and waiting for them to get cold and go home; that didn't work, as the kids would stay around until their faces were frostbitten and they were barely able to run on their cold feet. The cook didn't help either, as he would give the kids cookies or other small treats when they crowded into the caboose to get warm. When confronted, the cook would simply say that those kids were cold and needed to get warm. Our swing boss (lead operator) would be literally pulling his hair out in total frustration.

One particular trip through Oxford House was one of the scariest experiences of my life. The snow was very deep that year, which made walking off the trail difficult. The tractors would normally stay on the trail, except when descending a hill. The heavily loaded sleighs would push hard against each other and the tractor going down the hill. The force that the weight applied would sometimes jackknife the sleighs if the hill was too steep. Going off the trail into the deep snow was an option that helped slow the sleighs down as they ploughed through deep snow that acted like brakes on each load. We had just passed the nursing station and a school when we started descending a long, steep hill; I went off the trail to take advantage of the deep snow. As I guided the tractor train down the hill, I kept looking back at the children riding on the sleighs and wishing that they would just sit still and quit moving about. I was always worried that the smaller children would fall off the sleighs and get hurt. Two boys were running from one sleigh to the other, and this meant getting off one sleigh and walking on the couplers that joined the sleighs. It was a cold day, and I was worried for their safety as the steel they were running on would be slippery and their frozen rubber-bottomed boots would have no grip. The heavily loaded sleighs were starting to push, and I had to concentrate on keeping the tractor in a straight line to prevent the sleighs from breaking away and causing them to jackknife.

I was over halfway down the hill when one of the boys disappeared from my line of sight with the second small boy right behind him. I held my breath and waited. Then that boy suddenly appeared on the next sleigh, smiling as he scampered to the side of the load to look back. I was so relieved to see him again, and I knew that if I yelled for them to sit down, they would only smile and continue playing. The little boy that was on the third sleigh was attempting to climb off the front of that sleigh and follow the first boy to the next sleigh. I saw him jumping down to the steel coupler between the sleighs, and suddenly, I noticed the surprised expressions on the faces of the other children who had been watching the two boys playing, and I knew then that something terrible had happened. One of the children shouted in alarm, indicating that the child had fallen off the coupler. Hearing that, my heart immediately felt hot and weak, and I suddenly had trouble breathing. I knew I could not stop until I was off the hill and on level ground, and getting there seemed to take forever.

By the time I was able to stop, I was trembling with fear at what I may find back on the trail. I imagined the grief the boy's parents would endure. I felt sick to my stomach as it knotted up with tension and grief, and I also felt angry at these kids who put themselves in harm's way just to ride these tractor trains. I uncoupled and quickly put the tractor into its highest gear, racing back to the location where I thought the boy would be. I made sure I stayed off the trail as I drove back up the hill. I didn't know what I would find when I reached him, and I was wondering if I should even try to move him once I located him since I imagined he would have been crushed after being run over by the two heavily loaded sleighs.

I suddenly saw a little hand moving in the snow and realized that he was still alive. My joy was short-lived when my thoughts brought me to the realization that he may not survive all the crushed bones in his little body that the two sleighs had surely left him with. When I reached him, I jumped off the machine and started digging him out, now in a state of panic. He started moving as I freed him from the packed snow, and I could see the horrified look on his face as he tried to get away from me. The terror I saw in his eyes reminded me of the many times I had been caught red-handed when I disobeyed, and I thought how strange it is how we are so quick to disobey and never consider the consequences of that disobedience. I held him down, trying to reassure him that he would be okay. I began to wonder if I was telling him the truth, as I didn't know the extent of his injuries. I held him close to calm him down and prevent him from moving, in case he was seriously hurt. I realized what he was saying through his tears was that he thought I was going to discipline him and he was begging me to release him. I assured him that no one was going to punish him, and when he heard that, he seemed to calm down. After I saw he was moving all his limbs and he told me he felt okay, I carried him to my tractor to race him to the nursing station to be checked over by a medical person. I lifted him onto the tractor seat for the ride, and it was then that I saw the smile form on his face. A ride on the tractor was only a dream for many of these kids, and this was like an answer to a prayer for him.

The nurse immediately took him in and examined him. She told me he was okay and that she was going to keep him overnight for observation and let his parents know where he was. Also, she now had a reason to keep him away from the tractor trains, at least for that day. I was very relieved to hear he'd stay off the tractor trains for now. As I was leaving, I met the mother running towards the nursing station. (News travelled quickly in these communities.) She stopped and asked me if her son was okay, and I informed her that the nurse thought so. She said she'd always dreaded this day would come and she had warned him over and over again about the dangers of riding on the tractor trains, but he wouldn't listen. As I left her after our talk, I couldn't help but think that, as a little girl, she was probably like her little boy, whose dream was to ride these trains.

I enjoyed watching and listening to the joyful sounds of laughter from the people riding on our trains; I understood the excitement they were experiencing. I had once been one of those kids when we lived in Oxford House. The tractor train rides were fun, and being on one was like being in heaven, as the excitement heightens with each mile. It was the one thing the kids looked forward to each season, and no matter how they were threatened, they wouldn't stop. One kid told me a ride was worth dying for, and watching them play around these moving sleighs, I believed he meant it.

A few days later, as we were again approaching the community of Oxford House, I saw that same little boy standing on the side of the road smiling at me as I went by. He and the others had walked 8.05 kilometres (5 miles) out to meet our tractor train. Once they'd heard our tractor trains coming, they'd immediately started walking and running to meet us. We tried changing our arrival times to after midnight and during school hours, and the excited group still met us outside their community. Sometimes these kids would hitch rides when we left as well, riding from 8 to 16 kilometres (5 to 10 miles) out of their communities then jumping off and walking home. They would often ask what day we would be returning or travelling through their community, as our next visit gave them something to look forward to. I remember the sad looks on the faces of these kids when I told them this was our last trip of the season and we would not be returning again this year. The first time I told them this, I didn't know they would ride out a few extra miles, refusing to get off the sleighs when we asked them to. We had to unhook one caboose and haul them back home. The temperatures were sometimes – 37°C (– 34.6 F), and some of them were not dressed to walk that many miles back in the dark. Once we got them back home, they all got out and thanked us for the ride. I believed this was the highlight of their winter activities, and I was sure they would spend the summer dreaming of their next tractor train ride, as I often had as a child.

The job was sometimes dangerous, but I would go back to it in a heartbeat if these tractors trains were still operating today. I always felt I was living my dream when I was working on those trains.

*Patrica Transport's Bombardier (snowmobile)
parked in their yard at Thicket Portage, Manitoba.*

*Tractor train sleighs being loaded to transport
a truck, lumber, and heating plant equipment.*

*A Caterpillar tractor D6 from a tractor train
parked in front of our house.*

*A tractor hauled wood for the store, our home, and other buildings in
Oxford House. The wood is delivered yearly on several sleighs. Notice
the people riding and running to catch a ride on the sleigh.*

Chapter 16
The Canoe Trains

D URING THE SUMMER MONTHS, my dad used canoe trains to haul the freight for the store in Oxford House. The freight consisted of canned foods, dry goods, hardware materials, and traps and snares that the trappers used. These canoe trains used the Hayes River system, which involved making many portages around many fast-moving rapids, beaver dams, and the occasional raging waterfall. The canoe routes crossed many lakes since the rivers did not always run in the direction of the communities where the stores were located.

These canoes were called trains because one canoe was powered with an outboard motor and pulled two or three other canoes behind it. Each canoe had a person who would steer the canoe, especially during a crosswind, so the canoes could be kept in a straight line. When coming to a stop, the driver of the lead canoe would gradually throttle down his outboard motor before shutting it off a fair distance from shore. The canoes would then be uncoupled and brought to shore one at a time, as sometimes there was limited room on the shore landing area because of rocks or bush that had not been cleared. Three or four of these trains traveled together, sometimes consisting of four canoes per train. Each canoe carried about 450 kilograms (1,000 pounds), causing the canoes to sit low in the water. Thus, some lakes could not be crossed on windy days.

Some years when the water was higher, fast-flowing rapids didn't need to be portaged, as the canoes could be pulled upstream along the shoreline using ropes. This manoeuvre saved time and labour.

The freight my father received was shipped from Winnipeg on large lake boats that crossed Lake Winnipeg. He stored the freight in his warehouse at Norway House until it could be forwarded on to Oxford House by canoe trains.

The majority of the food was packaged in tins and cased in wooden boxes. Butter was also shipped in tin cans and cased in wooden boxes for shipping, so it didn't have to be kept cool to prevent spoiling. The flour, sugar, fabrics, and clothing materials were packaged in canvas or burlap bundles. The wooden boxes made it easier for handling, especially when carried along the portages on men's shoulders or in backpacks. Some of the men could haul hundreds of pounds on their backs along the portages. These backpacks had two straps that went around each shoulder and one long strap that went around the forehead called the tumpline, which supported the weight as the man leaned forward for balance. The men made it look easy, especially when they could literally run with the loads on their backs. The men carried the canoes on their shoulders during the portages.

Robinson Portage was the longest portage between Oxford House and Norway House, and it had a light railway track that spanned the full length of the portage built by the Hudson's Bay Company during the early fur-trading era. A flat-deck railway car hauled material along this portage. Once the men had loaded the rail car, they pushed or pulled the car along the portage, using ropes to control the speed as they descended down the gradual slope towards the river. They would make several trips until all the canoes and freight had been portaged. The women and children on these trips got to ride on the railcar to prevent delays since they did not travel through the bush as fast as the men. Often the men carried the canoes along the portages to speed up the crossing.

I travelled every summer on these canoe trains that were hauling my father's freight into Oxford House. I must have been about five or six years old when I went on my first trip. We started off from Oxford House one early morning when the weather was perfect. There was a gentle breeze blowing, just enough to keep the mosquitoes and flies from bothering anyone. I sat with my mother in one of the canoes, and the day passed quickly as we crossed Oxford Lake. Mom pointed out the many reefs along the way. Some of these reefs could be seen from a distance as the water splashed against their flat sides, and then there were those reefs that were lurking one inch below the water surface and would not be noticed until one was upon them. She explained that many of the people ran aground on these rocks when they were using outboard motors. She said that those who hit the rocks were not familiar with the lake, and I think she was referring to the Indian Agency employees and the Hudson's Bay personnel in Oxford House. We saw some of the most beautiful patterns on the lake shore, caused by many years of erosion. The one picture that remains in my mind was a distant shoreline Mom pointed to. She said it was called "Looking like a Doorway" in Cree. I could see an opening in the distance that looked like an entrance way. As you got closer to this site, the doorway disappeared. It was like an invisible door that one could only access from a distance. This reminded me of some of the friends I had. They would talk and share their experiences from a distance. But when you got close enough to look into their eyes, they would run away and disappear. It was hard to become good friends with some of these kids because of their shyness, and I knew they wanted to have friends. I learned not to look directly into the eyes of these shy kids as it was very hard for them to talk when the listener was looking at them.

The shore lunch was fun since we got to run around while the canoes were being hauled up around the falls and onto a river that would take us into Windy Lake. Some of the men did a little fishing at the falls and caught some of the biggest northern pike I have ever seen. After lunch, we were on our way up the river; then we crossed Windy Lake. Once we had crossed Windy Lake, we camped for the night. We had time to bathe and freshen up before going to bed in a tent that was set up near the canoes. I enjoyed the camping part most of all, as I could visit the people as they sat around their campfires telling stories.

The next morning, I awoke at 5:00 a.m. for breakfast, and most of the people were already awake and having breakfast. I would have preferred to stay at that location instead of moving on. One of the men would often set a short fishing net in the lake upon arrival at these stopping points, and it would be removed the following morning, providing fresh fish for the day. We next crossed Opiminegoka Lake, Logan Lake, and Robinson Lake, which was the final lake we would cross on the Hayes River system. The trips across the lakes were long, and the drone of the outboard motor along with the sound of the water rushing past the canoe bottom would often lull me to sleep within minutes of laying down my head. The waterways we travelled on were very interesting; we often saw many different types of birds and animals along the shorelines. Sometimes we would surprise a moose feeding on the underwater vegetations as we came around the bend in the river. It was funny to see him scramble out of the water and run off into the bush.

The last portage we would make was the Painted Stone Portage, which would take us off the Hayes River system and onto the Echimamish River. We would see a number of large beaver dams that we needed to cross before reaching Hairy Lake; then we'd head down the Echimamish River onto the Nelson River. The last stop we would make was at Sea Falls before reaching Norway House. This would be the last rapids we would have to cross to get to the upper side of the river. The falls were on the east channel of the Nelson River, and once across the falls, we would stay on the river into Norway House. We would start seeing houses as we passed Rossville on our way into Norway House. The people would come out of their houses to look at our canoe trains passing by. They were probably wondering where we had travelled from since the same approach could be made from Cross Lake, Island Lake, or Gods Lake, as well as Gods River or Oxford House. We knew Norway House as "Keenosayo Seepie" in Cree.

The following day would be a day of rest, as everyone visited relatives or friends before loading the canoes for the trip back to Oxford House. My mother and I would stay in Norway House and Rossville for a couple of weeks visiting her mother and family who lived in Rossville.

The men on the canoe trains returned to Oxford House with their canoes fully loaded with freight. My mother and I would return to Oxford House on a chartered aircraft two weeks later. The airplane was a Bittern Norseman aircraft that operated out of Norway House. This plane had large pontoons and operated on the lakes and rivers. There was very little room on the aircraft, as Dad always had it loaded with freight, leaving a minimum amount of room for Mom and me. The flight home took about an hour, and it was a very happy hour for me, as I loved flying in an airplane.

A canoe train unloading freight at a portage.

A member of a canoe train team hauling freight over a portage.

A canoe train preparing to depart Oxford House for Norway House.

A canoe train going to Norway House to pick up freight. The towing canoe is pulling five empty canoes. The crew all ride together in one canoe as the empty canoes do not need steersmen.

This photograph was taken from the towing canoe. The canoes are loaded with freight for Oxford House. Each canoe has a steersman.

A loaded canoe being pushed off shore after crossing a portage.

A shy little girl poses in this picture while the canoes are being unloaded to cross a portage.

A canoe train unloading canoes to portage.

Chapter 17
To Selkirk and Home Again

M Y FIRST TWO YEARS of schooling were in a day school at Oxford House, Manitoba. By then, nearly all the children I'd grown up with had been sent away to residential schools. Many of these children from the reserve would have been seven years old when they first left our community. The federal government's policy was that every Indian child from a reserve must attend a residential school; this program was fully funded by the government.

My father had made arrangements for me to go to a school in Selkirk, Manitoba, where my sister, Nellie, was already enrolled in a high school. This would be my first time leaving home without my parents. The joy of hearing that I would be travelling by airplane overshadowed all thoughts of being separated from my parents. I probably figured I'd only be gone for a short period since I was never allowed to be away from home for very long. Besides, all the other kids had gone somewhere else to go to school, so I just thought this was normal. In addition, Nellie would be travelling with me, as she was returning to continue her classes.

I was about ten years old, and Nellie was about sixteen. We both stayed in a boarding house, which was very comfortable. I liked our landlady, Mrs. Corrigal, whom I felt comfortable being around. Nellie and I had our own room, so we were able to stay together. She made sure I was awake early every morning, and we always had breakfast together before I left for school. I was very comfortable living there, and Mrs. Corrigal was a very good host, who was always cheerful. I didn't know then that this woman would become a part of my life that I would always cherish.

I believe my father sent us off to school in a southern town for two primary reasons—to learn to speak English and to be exposed to other cultures we were not yet aware of. During my father's childhood, he was exposed to many cultures and people that he admired and befriended; the couple who had adopted my father moved often since his father was a Methodist minister. Dad wanted his children to learn what he had learned and have similar experiences. The education we would receive would open to us the opportunities to compete economically and technically as adults.

I made friends with the local kids very quickly; rather, I should say that the neighbourhood kids came and invited me to play with them, so we became friends. The kids tried teaching me to ride a bicycle and to play games I'd never heard of before. I must have been a novelty to them, as I got a lot of attention. I didn't speak their language, and they all tried to help me learn to communicate with them. I never once felt discriminated against, as they all wanted me to be their friend. I was invited to every birthday party in the neighbourhood, and I was starting to enjoy my new life in Selkirk. My new friends and I went to see movies as a group every Saturday afternoon at the local theatre.

Mrs. Corrigal worshipped at the Presbyterian Church in Selkirk, where Nellie was a member of the church choir. I sat with Mrs. Corrigal during services, and she made sure I got to meet the members of the congregation. The Knox Presbyterian Church was Selkirk's first church congregation. I learned that the church had begun in a small log cabin on Eveline Street and evolved into the Gothic Revival structure that stood today. When I first saw this church from the outside, it reminded me of buildings I had seen in books that my father had. The initial structure was built in 1876. It was expanded in 1960 for the second time in its history. When I attended this church in the early 1950s, it was much smaller than it is now. The interior chapel was very beautiful, displaying the artistic skill of its builders in those early days. Pointed arch windows and doors and stained glass windows that permitted the sunlight to shine through, displaying the many colours of the glass, were among the building's highlights. During the evening services, the lights from inside the building reflected off the stained glass, thus directing one's attention to the beauty of this artwork. As a child, I spent many hours staring at these windows; I thought they had to be the most beautiful windows in the world. The artwork on the windows must have taken months to complete. The woodwork on the interior, which was highly detailed, also displayed the artistic skills of the builders, and the carved wooden pews were very comfortable.

This first winter away from home seems to have faded from my memory, as I don't remember much else of what I did that first winter. I don't believe I made much headway in my education since I was having a hard time learning the language and the culture of my new environment. I believe the sole purpose of that first winter was to expose me to this new world that was to become a part of me. I was never discouraged from speaking my language with my sister or with Mrs. Corrigal's friend who spoke a little Cree. Mrs. Corrigal would spend hours teaching me to speak English; I appreciated the time she spent doing this.

At the end of that first school year, we travelled home on a CNR train to Ilford, Manitoba, and then from there, on a small Tiger Moth aircraft to Oxford House. It was good to be home again, and I would forget most of what I'd learned in Selkirk that winter. I was glad to see our family dog, Duke, who would have a playmate once again. I often wondered why I didn't retain the memories of that first winter away from my parents; maybe my emotions blocked out the memories, as I am sure I would have been homesick during the first year. On the other hand, my sister and Mrs. Corrigal did such a wonderful job of keeping me occupied during that first winter, probably preventing my longing for home from becoming unbearable.

I thoroughly enjoyed my summer holidays, spending time with family and friends, fishing, swimming, and boating. As the beginning of August approached, I would soon be having my eleventh birthday.

I awoke to the sound of my mother and father talking in the kitchen. I quickly jumped out of bed to join them. My dad was usually gone to work by the time I awoke in the mornings, so I didn't often see him at the breakfast table. When I arrived, they were having their morning tea. My mother seemed to be in a serious mood, so I wondered what had gone wrong, thinking possibly one of our neighbours had fallen ill. I knew something was up, as these kinds of meetings at the kitchen table only took place when I had done something wrong or something important had happened. I was having my breakfast when my dad asked if I'd slept well and what my plans for the day were; thus, I knew something I did had not precipitated the meeting, which was a relief.

Once I completed my breakfast, my father looked at me and informed me that I would be travelling to Selkirk, Manitoba, to attend school and that I would be travelling alone. He asked if I was okay with that and told me he'd made arrangements to have the pilot look out for me on the trip. *Of course, I was okay with that arrangement!* I was very excited at the prospect of getting another plane ride. Dad told me that, once I arrived in Lac du Bonnet, he had friends there who would meet me and take me on to Selkirk. Once in Selkirk, I would be staying with other friends of his, who would look after me while I went to school. He then asked if I would like to learn to speak and write English. I told him that Bill was trying to teach me and that I liked learning the new words. I informed him that I thought maybe I could learn enough to someday be able to talk to Bill in the new language. I didn't tell him that Bill had only taught me my first two English words.

The summer went by so quickly, and the next thing I remember, Dad was reminding me that I would be travelling back to Selkirk *alone*. I never thought much about the school part, as all I could think of was being able to ride in an airplane; this had to be the highlight of my life! During that last week at home, my mother was especially quiet, and she would hug and hold me more than usual. She also planned more activities for us so that we spent more time together. I liked that, as I loved to show off, and she was always so thrilled when I showed her my newly acquired skills, whatever they were.

My last week at home seemed to take forever, as I waited for my departure day. I even thought that maybe time had stood still and this day would never arrive. I was really looking forward to another plane ride south. I remember that last morning very well, and even after the many years that have gone by, I can still see and hear the sights and sounds of that morning when I close my eyes. I had gotten out of bed earlier than usual; the skies were clear, and a gentle breeze blew in from the southwest. There was much excitement in our house that day, as many of my friends came by to say good-bye. My mom was packing my things. I couldn't help her, as I couldn't even think straight from all the excitement. She often stopped to cry and give me another hug. In my excitement I never realized how much pain she would be going through after I was gone. She had given me money, which she pinned in my sock so I wouldn't lose it. She made me lunch to take on my journey so that I could eat when I got hungry. My mother and I, along with our dog, Duke, walked slowly down to the lake, where my father and John were waiting. We all got into the boat for the trip across the lake to the Hudson's Bay dock, where the plane docked on arrival. The sun was strong, and I could feel its heat even as we traveled across the lake with the wind in our faces.

We parked at the dock, waiting for the mail plane to arrive, along with the people who had gathered to meet the plane to see who was coming or going. Sometimes relatives were on the plane travelling south and the visitors would be able to visit with their loved ones while the plane was being loaded and unloaded. The water gently lapped against the boards on the dock, and the people talked excitedly as they were waiting for family members to arrive. My mother kept reminding me to eat my lunch when I got hungry and that there was enough food in my lunch bag for two meals, as we would not arrive in Lac Du Bonnet until later that evening. My dad gave me instructions on what to do when I arrived at the other end and who would be meeting me there. If the people were not there when I arrived, I was to stay with the pilot and he would make sure I was looked after. I sat in the boat waiting with Mom and Dad. My dad seemed to be comforting my mother, and I wondered why she acted so agitated. She had been very quiet all week, crying a lot, and I didn't even realize that my going away was the cause of it. I stayed with her in the boat, even though I wanted to get out and play with some of the kids who were on the beach by the dock. I had decided that my mom was not well and she needed me to stay with her.

Little did I realize that life as I knew it was about to come to an abrupt end. I would not have the comforts of home with my parents as I had grown accustomed to enjoying during those cold winter months. My mother would become someone I remembered as if in a dream, and my heart would be torn apart over and over again, as I longed for her gentle hugs that often comforted me. Most of all, I would miss the closeness we enjoyed as mother and child in the days ahead. I believe now that my childhood days ended that day when I left home.

My dog was allowed to come with us on the boat trip across the lake, and he stayed with me and Mom in the boat. I think he knew something was wrong, as he was whining a lot and putting his head on my knees. When I was sick with the flu or a cold, he would often lay his head on me as a way of comforting me during my illness, and here he was doing just that when I was healthy and not sick. I think he was aware of my departure.

The plane finally arrived and the level went up a couple of notches on my excitement scale. I could smell the heat of the engine; airplanes had a certain type of smell because of the fuel they used. When the pilot opened the door, he remained in his seat, and I could hear the gyro on the instrument panel spinning loudly, as it continued to wind down in its rotation. The pilot unloaded the passengers and their baggage, and then he unloaded a dozen mailbags and some freight. I can still hear the excited chatter of the relatives meeting their loved ones, who'd arrived from various locations.

Finally, when all else was loaded, the pilot came over and talked to Dad, and they called me to let me know I was to board the plane. Suddenly, my mother didn't want to let me go, as she just wanted to give me that one more hug. The pilot was being very patient as he waited for Dad to persuade my mom to let me go. I am sure this pilot had seen many mothers refusing to let their children go when the time came for the kids to board the plane. My mother walked with me to the plane, and my dad lifted me onto the plane. We said our good-byes as the pilot helped me buckle my seat belt and made sure it was adjusted right, instructing me not to undo the belt until he told me to. My dad was holding my mom, as she was now crying out loud. My heart was torn apart to see my mother like this, and I think I was trying to unbuckle my seat belt when she told me to stay and be a good boy and listen to the pilot; and with that, I obeyed. I didn't realize then how heartbroken my mother was to lose her youngest child.

I was seated at the back of the plane by the rear main door, so I had a larger window on the door from which I could look out and enjoy the view. The plane was pushed away from the dock and the aircraft engine started, and we taxied out into the open lake for the take-off. As I looked out the window, I saw my parents one last time standing on the dock. My dad still held my mom as they both waved at me, and I waved back. My dog stayed in the boat, probably waiting for me to come back.

My excitement immediately returned when the plane turned to prepare for take-off. The plane's engine revved up the RPMs, and the plane bounced on the water as it increased speed. I could see one of the rudders located on the rear of the pontoon rise up out of the water as the pilot pulled them up for take-off. The water spray from the floats created a rainbow in front of the wings, which was a spectacular display of nature's beauty. I watched the pontoon on my side of the plane plough through the water as the aircraft accelerated in speed, the pilot attempting to get the floats up on the step and finally lift off. The pilot looked back at me and smiled, and I felt good knowing I was riding in an airplane. The time of departure was about 10:00 a.m. The sound of the engine was quite loud on take-off. Then the noise level was reduced somewhat as the pilot throttled down to cruising speed. As we climbed above the lake, I looked down and saw our home one last time; the sunbeams danced off the water surface on the lake around our home, which was located on a peninsula. I looked at the water surface on the lake, and I could see the reflection of the white clouds on the still water in the sheltered bays as it reflected the sky view. I had never seen anything so beautiful, and to think that I had been swimming in that same water; I felt truly blessed.

The mail plane I was on would stop at many communities before finally arriving in Lac du Bonnet. Our first stop was at Gods Lake Narrows. Then we moved on to Gods River, which was across the lake from the narrows. Next we headed to Island Lake. Some people boarded the plane at these locations, while others disembarked at their final destinations. I could see the relief on their faces at seeing their loved ones again. We continued landing at more of these communities, and I was thoroughly enjoying the plane ride. I must confess that, at this point, I had not thought of home. There was so much to see and hear, and I was still excited about the plane ride; it seemed that I could not get enough of it. The people on the plane were very friendly, and some asked who my parents were. When I told them, they all knew who my dad was. My father was a businessman who travelled throughout the north trading with the trappers in the area. He would have dealt with each family as he went about his business. Many of his customers became good friends, and he seemed to know everyone in the many communities I visited.

In one community, a woman and several children who were going to a hospital in Winnipeg boarded. The woman must have been very sick, as she kept throwing up blood into a quart-sized carton that the airline supplied for motion sickness. The container was similar to the milk cartons we find in the grocery stores today. I felt such compassion for her as I sat listening to her telling someone about her pain and about having to leave her family behind. I wondered if she would ever see her family again, as I knew they could not afford the plane ride to come and visit her. I'd heard from others that the cost of these plane rides was very prohibitive, especially for someone without an income.

One of the boys on the plane had a very colourful badge pinned on his chest; I didn't realize then that it was a badge showing his final destination. The fancy, bright colours impressed me so much that I just had to have it. I got to talking to him, and I made an offer to buy the badge from him. He explained that he was not allowed to remove it. My mother had given me some money for my trip, and she had hidden this money in my left sock, so I knew I could raise the price, as I was willing to pay whatever I needed to get that badge. I spent hours trying to convince the boy to sell me his badge. He kept telling me he was instructed not to lose that badge, as he would need it when he arrived at his destination. I am sure I even begged him to sell me his badge but without success.

It was late in the afternoon when I started feeling hunger pains. I hadn't eaten since breakfast that morning at home. I dug into my bag to retrieve one of the sandwiches for myself. As I started to eat, I noticed the boy staring at me with a keen interest in what I was eating. He told me he was very hungry, as he had not eaten since breakfast that morning. I was immediately aware of my bargaining leverage on the subject at hand. I told the boy, who was staring at my sandwich, that I would be willing to give him one dollar plus a sandwich should he consider trading for his badge. He immediately said no, so I quietly continued eating my sandwich. I was nearly finished eating my first sandwich when he asked if I had any more sandwiches. I informed him that I still had two sandwiches in my bag. He said that, if I gave him the two sandwiches and the dollar, I could have his badge. I was so overjoyed to finally get my prize that I gave him my two sandwiches, a drink, and the dollar. I pinned the new badge on my chest for everyone to see. I must have spent the next hour giggling to myself and admiring my new fancy badge.

The weather had changed along the way, and we had to wait in one community for the weather to clear. Then we were on our way again. The short delay due to the weather forced us to stop at Little Grand Rapids for the night. I shared a room with the pilot at the hotel in the community. I must have slept well that night, as he had to wake me the following morning for breakfast. I noticed that everyone on the plane had stayed at the same hotel. I was comfortable with the kindness of our pilot, and I never imagined that, someday, I would be flying with him as his co-pilot on an Otter aircraft when I would start flying as a commercial pilot in 1975.

Our plane departed from Little Grand Rapids that morning at about 9:00 a.m. As we approached the southern part of Lake Winnipeg, I could see the long roads and vehicles travelling on them. When two vehicles met on these roads, I was sure they would hit one another since the road looked so narrow from the air.

The pilot informed us that we would be landing at our final destination in a few minutes. I got very excited when I heard that, as I was looking forward to the vehicle ride into Selkirk and the opportunity to meet the people who would drive me there. The plane landed in Lac du Bonnet on the river, and my excitement heightened as we taxied towards the dock. I noticed the marshes along the way to the dock, and I thought that the water must be shallow in this area as it looked like the shallow bays at home. We taxied slowly, and the dock seemed far from where we had landed. Once the plane was docked, the dock hands secured the plane to the dock and installed a stairway for the passengers to disembark.

When it was my turn to get off the plane, two men who were waiting off to the side came to the bottom of the stairs. As I approached them, they looked at my badge closely, and one of the men took me by the arm and led me to a waiting van. I looked for the pilot to thank him for his kindness, but he had gone into the airline's building to deliver his papers. Someone had gotten my bags from the plane and loaded these into the van as well. I was then driven directly to the *Selkirk Mental Institution*!

Chapter 18
Returning to Selkirk

T HE SELKIRK MENTAL INSTITUTION had a person on staff who could speak Cree, as most patients from the north couldn't speak English. I was glad to hear that I would be staying in this nice building for a while. The worker who spoke Cree showed me to my room; it had a few toys for me to play with. She explained that the doctor would be coming to see me and spend some time with me tomorrow. I didn't ask her the reason for the doctor's visit, although I wondered why he wanted to see me.

That evening, I ate my supper, which was delivered to my room, and later that evening, I was served an evening snack. The snack wagon had juices; milk; cookies; and warm toast with jam, peanut butter, and honey, which were my favourites. I couldn't believe the service in this place, and I even had a choice between juice, milk, or hot chocolate! I was truly in heaven. I was getting to really like this place; being served meals in my own room was very special. The part I liked best was having all those toys to play with in my room. I spent all my time playing with the toys, until I was told that it was bedtime. My bed was very comfortable, and it had these soft, white sheets that felt cold when I first got into bed. I was used to having flannel sheets in the north.

The doctor arrived the next morning with an interpreter; the interpreter explained that she would be helping the doctor to speak with me. I continued playing on the floor with a Greyhound bus that was included with all the

154

toys. They didn't seem to mind me continuing to play with the bus on the floor as they asked me many questions. Later that day, I met another doctor who checked my eyes and ears and listened to my breathing. The lady who spoke my language told me that the last doctor had told her I was fine, and I replied that that was good. The first doctor who saw me came back the following morning. He asked me a few more questions and had me play with some blocks by putting them back into their proper slots. I was able to do this quickly, as I had a similar set of toys at home. I enjoyed playing these games, and the doctor would sit there and just stare at me as I continued to play. I answered all the questions the interpreter asked on behalf of the doctor. This doctor came to talk again after lunch, and the interpreter told me that that doctor was puzzled, as he'd mentioned that there was nothing wrong with me. I replied, "That's good."

On the third morning, this same doctor came back with another doctor, and I answered all their questions through the interpreter. They both watched me as I played with the toys they had brought, and I was enjoying all the attention from these people.

Later on near the end of the day, the interpreter informed me that a boy was missing in Lac du Bonnet and the police were not able to locate that missing boy. He'd apparently disembarked from an airplane just like the one I was on. I didn't reply since I was only interested in playing with all the toys.

Later, the interpreter was standing there talking to another woman when she mentioned a name that was the same as mine. I looked up. She noticed that I had stopped playing and looked up at her when she had said "Morris." She asked me if my name was Morris, and I said yes. She left in a hurry. When she returned, I was having my evening snack.

The interpreter informed me that I would be leaving with a policeman, who would take me to my new home in Selkirk, where I should have gone when I first arrived. I didn't question her statement, as I was so disappointed that I would not be staying in that nice building. I only wondered why I was being moved, and I never asked.

The large policeman arrived, and I went with him in his police car for a drive into Selkirk to my new home. I wondered why every policeman wore the same clothes as the others. I enjoyed riding in his new police car, and it was getting late in the evening so he turned on the lights. The dash lights on his car lit up so beautifully that I couldn't stop staring at them; I had never seen anything so beautiful.

When we arrived at the place that I would call home for the next few years, I met Mrs. Corrigal, whom my sister and I had stayed with the year before. She took me to my new bedroom upstairs, and I went to bed wondering where I would end up the next day. I saw two other men there; I was the only child in this house. This trip had been very exciting so far.

The next morning, I woke up early when Mrs. Corrigal called me to come downstairs for breakfast. Later, she helped me unpack and put my clothes away in the cabinet drawers. This would be the beginning of our wonderful friendship. She took me to several homes during those first few days so that her friends could meet me. Back at her home, we would sit outside in her backyard on warm days when the sun was strong. Sitting in the backyard just to enjoy the fresh air and the warm sun became our favourite pastime during those warm days. We would talk about school and families, and she never interrupted me when I talked about Oxford House or Norway House. I always felt good after our talks. I enjoyed listening to her stories about her life and her favourite pastime, gardening. I was never afraid to bring up subjects that concerned me, as she made me feel like I was the most important person in her life. I got to trust her very quickly, and she would often correct me when I was wrong. She did it in a loving way that made me appreciate her. We spent many hours together weeding the garden. Then we would reward ourselves with fresh-cooked corn on the cob from her garden. Hers was the sweetest corn I have ever tasted.

Not long after I arrived, Mrs. Corrigal started teaching me English. She kept repeating words, which I also repeated. She signalled with her arms and hands a lot when talking, so I was able to understand what she wanted me to do. She was preparing me for school by giving me speech classes. Soon, I would be in school, where I would get to meet more kids. Charlie, the handyman, also helped me with schoolwork and with English, and he was very good with the crossword puzzles he found in the newspapers.

After several days had passed, I started feeling homesick and wanted to go home. Mrs. Corrigal caught me crying several times, and she was able to comfort me by spending time playing with me in the yard. She showed me how to run a push lawnmower to cut the grass, and I enjoyed this very much. Some of her friends paid me to cut their lawns. I was excited about being rewarded for the job and about being able to purchase my own ice-cream cones and candy from the local candy store. Mrs. Corrigal helped me develop a habit of keeping busy and keeping my mind occupied. She did all she could to keep my mind occupied; she even allowed me to keep a couple of pigeons in the coal shed, which a kid from across town had given me as a gift. I spent many hours with these pigeons, with the understanding that I would keep the pens clean and the pigeons well fed.

The coal for the house furnace was delivered to the main floor of our coal shed; I kept the pigeons on the upper part of this shed. A large coal truck brought the coal, which came in large billets that needed to be broken into smaller pieces. Charlie showed me how to do this by using a sledge hammer, as I was always helping him anyway. The coal needed to be broken down into smaller sizes for easy handling since it had to be hauled to the basement furnace through the basement window. Once I learned how to do this, I helped Charlie break up the coal billets. I would sometimes go out to the shed after supper to break coal and place it into stockpiles for the days ahead. Charlie was always impressed that I could do this. He very seldom had to break the coal billets after that, as I kept a stockpile of down-sized coal for him when he came. The work kept me occupied as my homesickness grew worse during the evenings.

I would often cry myself to sleep silently in my room after I was in bed. I didn't want Mrs. Corrigal to know, as it would make her sad, and I liked her when she was happy. She was a very good person. Eventually, my homesickness got so bad that I would be crying during the daytime. Mrs. Corrigal tried everything to keep my mind occupied. Her sons and daughters from Winnipeg often came to visit her with their families, and this was the highlight of her week. Her children's families accepted me, and this made me feel like I was part of the family. I started looking forward to their visits on the weekends. Her sons and daughters were very good to me and treated me like their little brother.

One of her daughters, Gwen, and her husband, Stan, were frequent visitors. Stan would spend hours playing games with me while we built mechanical models on my mechanical set. Once we made a Ferris wheel that actually worked; it had a wind-up motor we used to turn the wheel through a belt system like my dad used on his sawmill. The excitement of our success lasted for days. I was so proud of our accomplishment. Stan purchased a large toy Greyhound bus for me like the one I had played with in the mental institution when I first came to Selkirk. I would spend many evenings playing with that bus. It had to be my favourite toy, and I received many gifts of toys from Mrs. Corrigal and her family.

Another daughter, Elsie, had two girls near my age. The sisters kept me busy playing games while their parents visited with Mrs. Corrigal. I enjoyed being with these girls; we always had a lot of fun playing with the games they would bring.

Bill and his wife, Gladys, lived a short distance downriver from Selkirk. Bill had little chickens on his acreage, and he and I would spend hours just watching these little chicks grow. I enjoyed holding the little chicks, as they were so soft and they would snuggle up in my hand and go to sleep. I sometimes stayed over on weekends at their house so Bill and I could stay up late during the cool nights fishing on the Red River. Gladys would have hot chocolate and cookies ready for us when we came home. I don't remember helping Bill scale the goldeyes that we kept, but I do remember throwing back the many small catfish we did catch. Other times when it was raining and we couldn't fish, we would all sit out on the veranda enjoying the hot chocolate. Later that summer, Bill saw that I was capable of handling the rowboat, so he would let me push off from shore and anchor out a ways to fish by myself. He would be so proud of me when I caught a few goldeyes.

Mrs. Corrigal had another son who lived right in town along Eveline Street, which ran along the Red River. This family had a son whom I would with play with out on the back fields along the river. I enjoyed being outside.

Mrs. Corrigal clearly noticed my lack of enthusiasm due to my homesickness, which was starting to overcome my best efforts to hide it. By this time, I had been in Selkirk for about two weeks. One morning, we went for a walk, and we stopped to talk to some of the kids playing on the street, whose parents she knew. I made a few more friends that day, and I even went home for lunch with one of the boys. My new friend from across the street spent a lot of time with me, and we got to be best friends. The next day, two brothers from down the street invited me to their house for a birthday party. This was exciting for me, as this was the first birthday party I attended in Selkirk. The party was for the younger boy, Lloyd, who turned eight years old that day. I enjoyed eating the cake, and their mother gave out prizes when we played games. Some of the prizes had coins in them, which we could use later to go to the movies at the town theatre. I spent many days with these brothers, and they became good friends of mine. Their parents were always kind to me.

Spending time with these new friends helped me finally overcome my homesickness. These new friends helped me learn to ride a bicycle. The day I learned to ride a bicycle was probably one of the happiest days I experienced in Selkirk. Some of my friends' families came out to cheer me on as I rode up and down the street showing off to my other new friends, who seemed so pleased that I could ride on my own. Now we were able to ride to the grocery store for ice-cream cones instead of walking. We also started going on long bicycle rides along the Red River. Later that fall, a few of us kids went on a long bike ride towards Winnipeg; we ended up turning back before we arrived in Winnipeg since we were all getting very hungry.

The more I got to know Charlie, the fonder I became of him. He made sure the bike I was using was oiled and cleaned, and sometimes he would adjust the spokes to ensure that it rode smooth and solid. He often joined us in the backyard to sip his tea after completing his handyman chores. He sometimes allowed me to help him with repairs around the house. I really liked that old gentleman.

Sundays, Mrs. Corrigal and I would spend part of the day at the Knox Presbyterian Church. Then we'd visit with her friends. Some of the people who went to our church brought their lunches in baskets to eat on the grass overlooking the Red River after the morning service. The local water ski club performed for the people; sometimes the skiers were just practicing, and this would entertain the local congregation. I never went hungry during those days, as everyone was always offering me food. I think I ate and enjoyed more of the pastry than anyone. I really enjoyed the people at the Knox Presbyterian Church, as they made feel like I belonged there with them. Dr. Dicki was the minister, and he was everyone's friend. When I sat alone in the church waiting for Mrs. Corrigal while she greeted her friends, Dr. Dicki would often come over and sit with me; he always made me feel so special. When I spoke to him in my broken English, he would listen like I was the most important person in the room. He made sure I was never alone, and he had me take part in the church's Christmas concerts. Later, I learned to play the trumpet and joined their brass band; I got to practice with the group for a Christmas concert.

I later got involved in the church youth groups. I joined the Cub Scouts, and the leaders always made me feel glad I was there. They would often take us to Lockport for sliding parties, which was a lot of fun; we sometimes ended the evening with a wiener roast on an open fire. The wieners tasted extra special this way. I learned so many things, like tying knots, which would come in handy later in life. I cherish the many memories I have of having been a member of that Boy Scouts troop.

Chapter 19
Going to School

THE DAY FINALLY CAME to register for school; the school board had told Mrs. Corrigal that I had to learn to speak English if I was to succeed in school. With the help of Mrs. Corrigal and the neighbourhood kids, I was able to speak enough English to get by. It was at this school that I would learn a very hard lesson about people who saw themselves as very important.

The school year prior to this, when I was with Nellie, I had attended a school near the edge of town. I attended the same school for about a week before I was transferred to a school near Mrs. Corrigal's home. I don't know why I was transferred, and I can only guess it was because of my lack of English skills. This new school had large, stone walls; obviously an old school building, it still had oak hardwood floors, and the clinks of footsteps echoed off the walls when anyone walked down the hallway. I remember looking at the large furnace heater vent that was located at the front of the room above the teacher. The wall around this vent had darkened from the coal- or oil-fired furnace fumes. The milk man made daily visits to the school bringing us small bottles of milk. We had a choice of white or chocolate milk, and everyone brought his or her fifteen cents to pay for the milk, which we received twice daily.

During the winter months, I was having trouble with one subject—mathematics. I was always getting low marks on this subject. I told Mrs. Corrigal about my problem. She had been noticing the marks on my report card and urging me to study more. I was studying, but I was not able to grasp the concepts we were working on. She told me she would spend one hour a day with me on this subject so that I could get a better mark on my last exam of the year, which was coming up. We sometimes spent two hours in the evenings and most of Saturday mornings and evenings working on mathematics. Charlie also helped me with some of the problems.

The methods Mrs. Corrigal used taught me to understand how the numbers worked, and I caught on quickly. The day of the spring exams came, and I felt confident when I was handed the exam papers. The students were separated so that there was an empty seat separating us from each other in all directions; this was to ensure that no one could cheat. I completed my paper and handed it in, and I was not the last one out of there; half the class was still writing. We were told we would receive the results in a couple of days. I felt confident I had done well on the exams.

The day our exam results were distributed, I was shocked to see I'd received a zero mark on my math paper. I went up to the teacher and asked why I had received a zero, and she said that I had cheated, as no one could improve his mark that quickly. My heart sank to a very low level as I left the class that day. I sat outside the school wondering what to do. I didn't want to go home to report that I had received a zero for a mark on maths. Most of the students in my class came to tell me they knew I hadn't cheated, and that brought me some comfort. But it didn't get my good mark back.

I brought the papers home and showed them to Mrs. Corrigal. She called the principal for an appointment the next day. The principal talked to Mrs. Corrigal and told her there was nothing he could do, as he had the word of the teacher against mine. I offered to write the exam for him to prove that I could pass. We left with the promise that he would talk to the teacher again.

The following afternoon, the teacher told me to stay in after school as she wanted to talk to me about my mathematical exam. When everyone was gone out of the classroom, she told me that she was sorry I had gone to see the principal and that she was not going to give me another chance to write this exam since she was to be married in two days. She didn't believe I could pass without cheating. I begged her to let me write the exam again, and I thought I had nearly convinced her when she told me she could not go back on her word, and that was final! She wished me better luck the following year, and I went home.

Mrs. Corrigal knew my feelings were hurt and my confidence in others was affected. She gave me the same advice my parents would have given me had they been there—to forgive and move on. She assured me that I had done all I could to correct the wrong by talking to the teacher and offering to rewrite the exam. We had many conversations over this subject; she was trying to help me overcome the negative feelings I was developing, as she knew my confidence in others was slowly fading. As we talked, I started realizing that the teacher was convinced she was right. That's when I forgave her. I knew I could not continue harbouring bad feelings towards her; doing so would only continue hurting me.

It turned out that I still passed the grade, as my marks were all high enough in the other subjects to get me into the next grade. The mark on my maths exam would have been 98 percent if it was accepted, which was the highest mark I had ever gotten on a maths exam. I never saw that teacher again since I was again transferred to another school the following year. That school was further out of town, and going there meant riding on the Beaver Bus Line's bus.

I was getting to know a lot of the people in Selkirk; I could go into most houses along the river and know the occupants in those houses, as they were all friends of Mrs. Corrigal. During the warm days in the fall and spring, I would often walk to and from the school, passing by the teams of horses and the teamsters on their way to or from work at the Manitoba Rolling Mills. The teamsters always had dirty faces from working with rusty, old metal, which would be melted down in the mill to make new steel.

I got to meet a lot of kids along the way to the school, and some of these kids attended the same school. One morning, I tore my pants playing on my way to school; I knew I could not return home, as I would miss school. One of my friends whom I usually walked to school with saw my torn pants and told his mother. She came out to have a look and invited me in so she could mend my pants. I was so happy to have my pants repaired, and no one noticed the tear, as she did such a good job on the repairs.

While attending this new school, I met two Russian boys who were just learning to speak English. They lived with their mother not far from the school. I often shared my lunch with them during the morning recess. I remember one day in particular, as it changed my eating habits for good. The boys invited me to their house for lunch, and I was just thrilled to get out of the schoolyard. We arrived at their small house, and they greeted their mother, who spoke very little English, in their language. She seemed surprised that her boys had invited a friend to their house for lunch. The boys explained that they had not told their mother in advance that they were inviting me to lunch at their house. The boys told me that she was just pleased that they had a friend. I asked where their father worked, and they told me they did not have a father, as he had died. I didn't know what to say after hearing that. I could not imagine what it would be like not to have a father.

The dinner table was set; they were having mushroom soup for lunch. I hated mushroom soup, and I would not eat it if my life depended on it! As I stood there wondering what I should do, I noticed that there were only three places set for lunch. One of the boys directed me to one of the places. I stopped and asked where their mother was going to sit. They told me she would do without, as she was giving me her portion. This was all they had to eat today, as they were very poor. I offered to pass, and they explained that I was their guest and they were sharing the little they had. I ate that mushroom soup like it was the best meal I ever had, and to this day, mushroom soup is still my favourite soup. I have never known people who were so generous and kind. I pray that these two boys grew up to be leaders of our nation, as we need ambassadors like that to make our nation strong.

Chapter 20
Going Home for Summer Holidays

THAT SUMMER—THE SUMMER OF 1956—after school was out, I was told that I would be going home to Oxford House for the summer holidays. I was very excited and relieved that I would not have to attend summer school that summer. I was really looking forward to the trip home to see my parents and friends!

My trip home would take a different route from the way I'd come. Instead of a plane ride, I would be on a large lake boat that hauled passengers across Lake Winnipeg to Norway House. The boat that I would be traveling on was called the SS *Keenora*. Tom, the boat's purser, looked after me on the trip across Lake Winnipeg. I remember the excitement I felt upon hearing the boat whistle advising passengers that the boat would be departing in ten minutes. The boat was facing south when it anchored to the dock to take on passengers and freight. The whistle finally blasted several times, indicating that the boat was departing. I watched as the loading ramps were removed and the boat's gates were shut. The large ropes that held the boat to the dock were all removed and neatly stored aboard.

The big boat vibrated when the engine started turning the propellers, and the boat moved away from the dock into the middle of the river. There, the captain cut the engine again to allow the boat to drift since it turned with the current on the river to head north to Lake Winnipeg. Once it completed the turn, the engine cut in again, and the speed quickly picked up. I was very excited to be on that boat. I stood on the top deck and watched the shoreline view and the many homes along the river, whose residents came out to watch and wave as we went by.

My amazement continued when I was told that supper was being served below and that I was to go and have my evening meal. This was exciting, as I could not imagine eating and travelling in a boat all at once. I was afraid I might miss something if I went below; I hurried so I could return quickly. After supper, a man played on the piano in the dining room, entertaining the passengers on board. There was a lot of excitement in the air, as we were getting closer to the big lake.

I shared a room with another boy directly across the hallway from the purser's cabin. I am sure they put us there so the purser could keep an eye on us. My roommate was an older boy who worked in the boat's canteen. As the canteen's keeper, he let me help serve the customers. I often thought we had a large cabin on that boat, but seeing it again many years later, I would be surprised to see how small it really was. Our cabin had running water and a sink for washing, which made it seem larger than the crew cabins. The toilets were located in a separate room further down the hallway. I didn't think I would be able to sleep that night listening to the vibration of the boat's propeller and engine, but I slept like a baby the whole night.

Somewhere in the middle of Lake Winnipeg, the boat's buzzers and whistles started sounding their alarms. We soon discovered that this was a drill, signalling us to abandon ship. Such a drill took place on every trip in order to ensure that the sailors on board would be able to get everyone off the boat safely should an emergency occur. At first I thought it was the real thing, and I was very afraid. It was my roommate who helped me put on my floatation device and took us to the location where the boats were being lowered. One boat was loaded with people and lowered to the water and then pulled up again. It turned out to be a learning experience for me, and I felt confident our sailors on board would look after us should we face a real emergency.

We continued sailing across Lake Winnipeg, stopping at the communities along the east and west sides of the lake. Our final destination on this boat would be Warren Landing, located at the mouth of the Nelson River on the north end of Lake Winnipeg. I did not get to see all the communities along the way, as the boat travelled twenty-four hours a day, and we stopped at some of the communities during the nighttime while I was asleep.

When we arrived at Warren Landing, we were transferred onto a smaller boat called *Chickama*. This small tugboat pushed barges loaded with equipment and freight down the Nelson River and across Playgreen Lake into Norway House, Manitoba.

My mother's sister, Mary, and her husband, Johnny, met me in Norway House. I stayed at their house for a night while waiting for the aircraft that would take me on to Oxford House the following day. Johnny worked for the federal government in Rossville; he was my favourite uncle. He was considerate, kind, and a very pleasant person to be around. Johnny was also a gifted violin player, and he would often play his violin to entertain Mary; their daughter, Elsie; and his dog, Napoleon. I, of course, was also privileged to be part of the audience. Johnny had a personality that could make you forget all your troubles when he thought you were homesick. Napoleon was a golden retriever, just like the one I had at home, and Napoleon would sing along when Johnny played the violin. Napoleon loved to play in the water, and he never grew tired of fetching sticks that I would throw into the lake. When I stopped playing to have a rest, he would get impatient and start barking until I threw another stick into the water. I would spend hours playing with this dog, and I felt safe with him by my side when we ventured far along the lake shore during our long walks.

The following day, Johnny took me to Fort Island, where I was to catch the mail plane going to Oxford House. When we arrived at the dock, the agent for Canadian Northern Airways informed us that the plane had been delayed by weather and that it should be along shortly. The plane was stranded somewhere up north and hadn't returned the day before. The agent said the pilot would depart for his regular schedule route once he returned and refuelled. In the north, when an airline tells you that the plane should be along shortly that could mean hours or days.

Johnny had to work that day, so he left me at the dock with the airline ticket agent to wait for the plane that was due to arrive shortly that morning. The agent stayed in his little shack while I waited on the dock. The day passed by quickly, and I took several walks along the shoreline. By this time, I was starting to feel hunger pains, and my stomach was often growling. It was now early in the afternoon, and still there was no sign of the plane.

Later that afternoon, I watched one elderly man cutting firewood for his house across the river channel on West Island. Once he completed his task, he sat outside his house on the front deck that was facing the river. His wife brought him a cup of tea while he rested. Once he emptied his cup, she came back out. They were having a discussion and often looked towards me. She finally went back into the house, and he got up and walked to the river, where he got into his boat and paddled across the river to where I was sitting. When he reached the dock, he spoke to me in Cree and told me his wife wanted to know if I had anything to eat, as she'd noticed I had been at this dock all day. I told him I had no food with me since I had expected to be in Oxford House by now. He said he and his wife wanted me to come to their house for dinner. I told him I worried I'd miss the plane if I left, as I was hoping to get home today. He said he would talk to the agent and find out when the plane might arrive.

A few minutes later, the agent came out and assured me that he would come across the river to get me should the plane arrive. With that assurance, I got into the man's boat, and we travelled across the channel to his house on West Island. When we arrived at his home, his wife served us a big meal. During the meal, the old man and his wife included me in their conversations as if I was a family member. I felt quite comfortable being with them. I would always remember these kind folks, who went out of their way to feed a hungry stranger. I never did find out who they where, and I felt terrible that I did not know their names when my dad asked who it was that had showed me such kindness. During my time at the couple's home, I had never thought of asking who they were as my parents may have known them. The image of these kind people sharing their food with me was burned into my memory to remain there for eternity. In years to come, I would meet many people along life's journeys, but this couple would always stand out fresh in my memory. Even to this day when someone shows me kindness, I immediately see this couple in my mind like it was only yesterday. For that, I am eternally grateful, and I will always treasure that memory. I discovered at an early age that the people of the north were hospitable, kind, and considerate. As a child growing up in the north, I never felt I was among strangers, even if I didn't know anyone.

The plane finally arrived around four o'clock that afternoon; once it was fuelled and loaded, we boarded for the flight home. As we lifted off the water and gained altitude, I was able to see Johnny and Mary's house in Rossville. By then, Johnny was working and probably didn't know I had waited all day for the plane. I am sure he went to check on me after work. I was so happy to be finally on my last leg of the trip home.

The plane landed in Oxford House one hour later, and Mom, Dad, and John were all waiting for me at the Hudson's Bay store dock, where the pilot dropped off the mail before going on to Gods Lake to complete his run for the day.

We departed, and my mother held me all the way home. She wanted to know everything. I was so happy to be home and just enjoyed the love and attention I was getting. I didn't tell her that there would be experiences that I would never share, like the incident when I first arrived in Selkirk and ended up at the Selkirk Mental Institution. People in Selkirk had told me that the incident would upset my parents if they found out, and they never did.

When we arrived at our dock, Duke was standing there waiting, and when he recognized me, he went into a frenzy, like he didn't know what to do with himself. He kept getting in my dad's way with his jumping around as Dad attempted to secure the boat to the dock. Finally, Duke jumped into the boat, and I was showered with his wet kisses. It was so good to be with him again. His excitement continued as we walked up the hill to our house, like he couldn't contain his joy at having this kid back home again. I sat with him that evening, stroking his head while I told my mom all that I had done while I was away at school. I didn't want that evening to end. I had dreamt and longed for these moments for a year.

The next morning, Duke was sitting by the kitchen door waiting for me to play fetch the stick or go for a walk—waiting to just be together. This would be the last summer I would spend with this dog; I would not see him again. My parents would move to another location while I was gone, and they would give Duke to an elderly couple in another community. I know he was well cared for, and he had the couple's many grandchildren to keep him occupied. The new owners lived near a lake, where he could swim and fetch the sticks their grandchildren would throw into the lake just to watch him swim. With those children to watch over, Duke would return each night to his new home, happy and tired at the end of another day. I will always believe that dogs are man's best friend, as they will love you unconditionally.

The summer went by quickly. I enjoyed many fun-filled days at home. My father took us on fishing trips and picnics on the lake. During this visit, I became aware that I was guarding my emotions, and I kept a distance from my mother's loving embraces. I didn't feel as comfortable knowing that this was just for a few weeks and then I would be leaving again to live among strangers whom I'd gotten to know as friends. I considered the Corrigals in Selkirk my other family.

There would be many lonely days ahead, when I would be away from my own family and dog, who I loved so much. But for now, I relished the sights and sound of my northern home—the home where I'd grown up.